DEGENERRATION
GAP

T0078254

DEGENERRATION
GAP

Jadd

PARTRIDGE
A Penguin Random House Company

Copyright © 2013 by Jadd.

ISBN: Hardcover   978-1-4828-1443-9
              Softcover   978-1-4828-1444-6
              Ebook   978-1-4828-1442-2

To order additional copies of this book, contact
Partridge India
000 800 10062 62
www.partridgepublishing.com/india
orders.india@partridgepublishing.com

Contents

Preface 7

Chapter 1 9
    "Shut up! Go away from here!"

Chapter 2 14
    What a smiling, sweet looking child! . . .—a Recap

Chapter 3 21
    Challenges of a mentally and physically
    handicapped girl

Chapter 4 25
    The Family's first trip to Goa

Chapter 5 46
    Predicament of a Mother—
    a Housemaker and the Focal Point

Chapter 6 61
    Mahesh a "A Jack of all trades"

Chapter 7 65
    The Changing Times

Chapter 8 84
    "Do not meddle in my life",
    "I am not a kid anymore"

Chapter 9 113
    "A friendship that Went Sour"

Chapter 10 141
    The Path to Success and Happiness

Preface

The contents of this book focuses on a small family and highlights the disparity in the mindsets of the parents and a growing elder daughter coupled with the pressures of handling another but younger daughter with disabilities in the fast changing society with a multitude of mediums of communication in terms of internet, swanky mobile phones, with myriads of features, the youngsters of today are in a league of their own with the parents being outdated and outpaced.

The book deals with a variety of difficult situations entailing a clash of mindsets of parents vis-vis children, having a disruptive impact on day-to-day life of the family. The objective is to engage the minds of the readers to throw open this subject so that we can undertake a serious introspection to try and thrash out an amicable solution and bridge this supposed generation gap which exists between elders and youngsters.

The effort in this is to cite numerous examples with which readers of different age-groups would be able to identify with. There are genuine attempts to make the book interesting to read as well. The title of this book ie "De-generration gap" should spur the minds of readers and would help all of us to evolve a harmonious atmosphere within the confines of our day-to-day family lives. We sincerely hope that the book would be a step forward to confront, resolve and win over these conflicts which we encounter in our lives.

Best regards,

Jadd

Chapter 1

"Shut up! Go away from here!"

Mahesh as the father was trying to help in counselling Shagun on her current preoccupations as a designer and the project she was handling at the prevalent point in time. Her impulsive reaction was "Shut up. Go away from here." Mahesh was, as usual, dumbstruck with mixed feelings on how to react. Surely, there was something seriously wrong with the relationship not mending at all.

Shagun is Mahesh's elder daughter who is today a qualified fashion designer aged 23 yrs and doing freelance projects. She has become egoistic, arrogant instead of humbling on the success she has got in which her parents Mahesh and Priti have had no role to play. On the contrary, she nurses a grudge against the parents for being over focused on her younger sister, Kiran who is a 17 yr old special girl with handicaps from childhood.

This is a small family today groping hard with the changing times but bereft of the harmony associated with a close knit family. The narration of this incident is to apprise the readers on the utter lack of communication and understanding which existed between the father and the elder daughter.

Let us now go back in time to understand the chain of events which led to this situation and the kind of efforts which were made to resolve the crisis which got created out of these occurrences. Mahesh had a mixed sense of fatherly anger as well as a realisation that the situation had inevitably gone out of hand. Impulsively, he reacted sharply at this reaction of Shagun. At this, she reacted "What can you do?"

On hearing this Mahesh was enraged and said "I will slap you hard and throw you out of the house".

Shagun reacted "I will call the police and malign you both badly" On hearing this, Priti came scampering and pulled Mahesh away and tried to cool him down.

Kiran, the younger daughter was highly crestfallen and did not know how to react. Though being a special child, she could guage the lack of harmony in the house.

Later in the evening, Mahesh reflected on what had happened, and felt very guilty and responsible for the situation. There is a slender difference between self control and parental guidance. Priti felt it as much as Mahesh that Shagun should respect her parents, it was equally necessary to genuinely determine the cause of lack of harmony in the family and why the growing daughter of 23 yrs should be so disregardful of her father, as highlighted above.

It was evident that Shagun nursed deep grudges against both her parents, which developed over years. Her outburst that day was one of the many which had happened earlier over the preceeding years, Mahesh and Priti were understandably more concerned about Kiran owing to her special needs. It is highly possible that Shagun subconsciously started feeling insecure in her earlier years, seeing that the parents were more inclined towards seeking medical help for Kiran.

Kiran was mentally lagging far behind girls of her age and needed help in walking specially on uneven surfaces.

A few years after her birth, she was able to walk around in the house, on her toes.

In order to correct this apparent anomaly, medical advice was taken and a surgery was recommended on the feet.

At such a tender age, it was a sight, post surgery, which was not easy to digest. It logically followed that the entire focus of the parents was to provide whatever solace that was possible to enable Kiran to take the surgery in her stride. However, the surgery which took place in year 2000 also perhaps represented the time when Shagun started feeling neglected and hence insecure. She was in the eight standard in school

While the parents were understandably preoccupied with taking care of Kiran, they did not realise that the behaviour of Shagun was changing for the worse and she was becoming increasingly irritable and disrespectful of them.

On the contrary, Mahesh and Priti also failed to understand the predicament of the situation and ended up harshly scolding Shagun for her unruly behaviour instead of giving her love and affection as well and also explaining the situation to her.

The going was tough on both the parents and they failed to do the balancing act in discharging their responsibilities towards both the children. With the passage of time, Kiran, post surgery, started bending her knees and her walking stance was unstable. It so emerged that the entire objective of getting the surgery done was defeated as she was now not walking on her toes but had started bending at the knee level.

There was a lot of resulting frustration at this development.

There was a lot of dejection at this and the disobedient behaviour of Shagun further worsened the situation.

Both Mahesh and Priti individually and collectively gave vent to their frustration on her. The atmosphere in the house was dismal. Mahesh and Priti felt that their individual karma of previous lifetimes was responsible for disharmony in the house. Both also realised that Shagun was not at fault and needed to be counselled appropriately.

Shagun, on the other hand, a growing girl of 12-13 yrs, at that point, was not mature enough to understand the mindsets of her parents. Time passed and the relationship between Mahesh and Priti on one hand and Shagun kept worsening. Shagun's academic performance in class deteriorated over time adding to the woes of the parents.

Kiran was growing up to be mentally challenged girl with physical disabilities as well. she continued to go to a special school with separate sections for special children.

This family of four was led by Mahesh who is a Chartered Accountant by profession, is doing a small trading business with a close friend as the other partner. The going is topsy turvy though Mahesh has been able to give a fairly comfortable life to his family.

Priti is a housemaker which is a more tedious job, managing a house as well demanding children.

As a family, they used to have dinner out in the club of which they were members apart from frequenting well known eating joints as well. However, this also changed over time as the increasing discord between the parents resulted in unhappy endings to outings.

In the meantime, Shagun became friendly with a young boy and her outings were mainly with him.

The frequency of their meetings increased, and so the famous saying "Familiarity breeds contempt" came into play. The friendship came to a bitter end. The positive in this was that kiran was increasingly attached to Shagun and despite being a special child was able to understand that Shagun's behaviour must improve vis-vis the parents. The parents both over heard Kiran, in her own way advising her elder sister to behave better.

All families have their own set of struggles and have to confront and win over them.

Chapter 2

What a smiling, sweet looking child! . . .—a Recap

It is year 1991! three years after Shagun was born. She grew up in these tender years as a sociable child, ever ready to recite poems in any gathering irrespective of the attention and focus on her. This was an indication to her parents of her future extrovertish being. As a parent, Mahesh was understandably circumspect about how she would adapt to a play school which based on the present day scenario, was a dire necessity in the run up to a full-fledged normal school.

Finally, the d day came and Priti as a dutiful mother was set to take her to the play school which was walking distance from the house. Very surprisingly, Shagun asked her mother, after a while, to go home and pick her up, when the school is over.

Priti came back home bearing a bewildered look on her face. On seeing this, Mahesh enquired about what had happened. Both of them were known to have created hell for their respective parents when they started going to school. Finally, it was time to pick her up from the play school. To her surprise and astonishment, she found a smiling Shagun, waiting for her, there. the teachers were profusely praising her and her friendly nature.!

Shagun too, was in high spirits! On being asked she replied "Mom, I have made friends and there were lot many things to play with" Mom was really dazed to see her level of confidence and her ability to mix with other children so quickly, on the very first day. Priti rang up Mahesh in office to inform him and he was surprised as well.

It is commonly seen that children in the age group of 3-5 yrs are rather shy and take time to mix with other children. There are other categories of children who are so petrified of staying away from their parents that they create panic in the morning everyday and cry and shriek on being taken to school.

Mahesh recollected his friend's son who used to wail at the top of his voice early in the morning everyday, during his early years in school. In other cases, mothers were known to hang around in school every day for a short duration, in the initial period.

Both the parents expressed their gratitude to the almighty, for being amongst a privileged few who did not face any problem whatsoever with their toddler going to school. There were quite a few friends who had taken counseling classes to know how to prepare their child to go to school. Some parents after going through harrowing experiences with their toddlers had to actually approach Padaetric doctors who specialise in handling of children, to guage if there was actually something wrong with their child for being so cranky in going to school.

Both Mahesh and Priti realised that Shagun's prompt adjustment in the play school would pave the way for her induction in a regular school, provided the tests were cleared.

Hence, time passed rather comfortably for them as parents. Finally, the time came for shagun's formal induction in a full fledged school which, too. was ½ km away from their residence. as a step in this direction, they visited the school to get the form and to understand the procedure as well as to know about the level of preparedness of the child.

In response to their queries, they were informed that it is a proper procedure which would entail not only the interview of the child for several rounds but of the parents as well.

There was a lurking fear of the possibility and quantum of donation which may be required to be given.

Therefore, it dawned upon Mahesh that he would have to keep a sizeable sum aside for this eventuality.

The pleasure of seeing their daughter grow and start school at the primary level, after a stint in play school was more than overshadowed by procedures and regulations followed by well known schools and was replaced by fear, apprehension as though an exam was required to be cleared.

Based on the briefing of the school authorities, Mahesh and Priti started the process of preparing their little Toddler of 4 yrs in terms of poems, names of fruits, animals, daily necessities etc. Likewise, they started updating themselves with basics, current affairs and general knowledge, relevant to that point of time. Finally, the day came and while Shagun bore her usual captivating smile, both the parents were highly circumspect.

On reaching the school, Shagun was whisked away to an adjoining room. The worried parents had to wait for their turn. Mahesh was basically questioned on the time he would devote to his daughter as a father while Priti was quizzed on her abilities to constructively contribute to Shagun's upbringing. Both the parents came out of the room in a disturbed state of mind, assuming that they had failed the test.

On the other hand, Shagun was all smiles when her test was through. Typically, they asked her to thank the teachers when it was time to leave. In response, in front of the teachers, Shagun chose to tell her mother "shut up". On hearing this, hey were dazed but the teachers all burst out laughing. The three walked out having been told that results would be declared one week later.

The trio was back a week later and were surprised that Shagun had been admitted to the school without any donation required to be given at all. Mahesh and Priti thanked the teachers for their help and cooperation., but were surprised to know the main reason for Shagun to secure her admission.

It was the "Shut up" which she said to the parents when the interview was over. This reaction coming from Shagun towards her parents surprised them all, conveying to them her self confidence, sense of independence. The teachers found that cute as well and not once did anyone of them point out her mis-behaviour with her parents.

Mahesh and Priti forgot about this trivial occurrence and were elated on the fact that they able to secure her admission to a reputed school, with ease. Little did they realise that a smiling toddler called Shagun would grow up to become a distraught, arrogant and egoistic lady with scant regard for her parents, as explained in chapter 1, though briefly.

The intention is not to point all fingers at her, as several other factors were responsible for the rift which got created for which neither the parents and her were responsible. These aspects have been time and again highlighted, with the objective of bridging the ever increasing gap as well.

Shagun's journey in school continued smoothly and she continued to get good grades till class 9th.

Thereafter, the father realised that she had a creative potential which would flower well if she got into a vocational course in addition to school rather than subjecting her to the rigours of academics only. This was a calculated gamble and worked out towards bettering her career prospects.

With the passage of time, Shagun got appreciation from from her teachers in college where she was pursuing her course in textile designing. Later, after completing this course she joined a Reputed Institute of fashion designing to do a course in fashion designing as well.

This combination of the two courses enhanced her profile and this helped her to train with wellknown designers as well as consultants as well. Her profile now looked further colourful and had an impact on customers who marketed and sold designer garments.

On the other hand, the professional progress she made in her initial career, was making her increasingly egoistic, arrogant with a sense of pride in having done so well so far. Since her line of activity was vastly different from that of her father, there were no real inputs from him, while Priti continued to be a house maker and could not counsel Shagun on her career.

As a consequence, she developed utter disregard for her mother and the fact that she was just managing the house. The father was a source of financial help on a day to day basis, which too was not satisfying enough for Shagun, as it emerged during the course of the brief communications the parents had with her. All that was being done for her was taken for granted by her as she found the parental help inadequate in comparison to what was being done by other parents.

Hence, Shagun was rapidly becoming self-centred without any basic bonding with her parents in terms of love and affection which both Mahesh and Priti had with their respective parents in the earlier years before marriage.

Notwithstanding this, Shagun did nurse a latent grudge as mentioned in chapter 1, regarding the over concern of the parents for the younger daughter ie her younger sister, Kiran. However, she has a strong bond too with Shagun, this was evident in the extreme concern which Kiran shows on a daily basis for her sister's needs in terms of her house hold reqts. This is despite the fact that Kiran is a mentally handicapped girl. with physical disabilities as well.

Let us now focus on Kiran's upbringing and what it takes to take care of a physically challenged girl.

Chapter 3

Challenges of a mentally and physically handicapped girl

Kiran was born in 1994, and was six years younger than her sister at that point of time. Shagun was eagerly looking forward to the arrival, so were the parents, as they felt that it was necessary that Shagun should not grow up to be lone ranger and sibling camaraderie is crucial for a balanced upbringing of a child. She also was very keen to have a younger sister. So be it! The delivery happened in the afternoon and all nears and dears present were elated at the news of the new arrival.

The coming days and months were extremely busy for Priti as she was completely preoccupied with Kiran. Time passed and it was a couple of months later when Priti realised that Kiran was not trying to sit or even trying to stand considering that she was nearly 1 year old. What followed was a series of tests which did not prove anything categorically. It was finally around 2 yrs when it got confirmed that Kiran's development was delayed both physically and mentally. The parents were told that her milestones were delayed in medical terms.

It therefore dawned upon both Mahesh and Priti that Kiran was emerging to be a special child and would require special care as well. The usual things which children start doing at the age of 2-3 yrs were not happening in the case of Kiran. However, her name itself means "hope" which meant that the parents had to be hopeful and be steadfast in their efforts to do whatever was possible at different intervals of time. Nevertheless, the commonly asked question ie "Why us" did have an impact on them. Initially, it is difficult for anybody to easily digest an occurrence like this.

The process of self pitying starts off which does not lead anywhere barring a sense of anger which, too, is inconsequential. The logic behind such realities obviously relates to our past lifetimes and is the result of negative karma which we have accumulated. This can be the only justification and rather than indulging in self-pity, such problems should be confronted and handled in a constructive manner.

As already mentioned in chapter 1, apart from her delayed mental milestones, she had a physical anomaly in terms of her walking on her toes. After a great deal of research it emerged that a surgery was required on the back of her heels which would straighten her walk, and make it more stable. On the contrary, the surgery worsened the situation as she started bending her knees. Earlier on, Kiran's walk was stable though she walked on her toes.

Henceforth, she could move around the house and would fall at times. But on uneven surfaces she could not manage independently, without a supporting hand to help her. The entire process from the time she was born, to this phase, post surgery, required increasingly more care and concern for her. Both Mahesh and Priti did not realise that they were neglecting Shagun in this process and were not devoting time to her.

This was alienating her from them Being human, they wrongly expected her to understand the situation. Although, with the passage of time the bond between the two sisters kept strengthening with the elder one ie Shagun doting on the younger one.

It was a complex situation with the parents giving more attention to Kiran and, understandably so. It was huge asking for the parents to fine tune the balance to such an extent that the elder one could have been completely satisfied. Hence, it was the parents who had to face the brunt of the irritable and disobedient behaviour of Shagun.

The parents individually and collectively ended up scolding Shagun for her mannerisms, an occurrence which worsened matters further. Shagun was ten years old at that time. and was in class 6. In school. This relationship crisis perhaps was also responsible for her deteriorating academic performance in school. The burdened parents were faced with another daunting task of arranging tuitions for her to come up to the desired level. in school.

The outings for a meal or a movie started turning out to be unpleasant with shagun being upset with something or the other. Time passed and the situation kept worsening, but to no avail.

Kiran started going to a special school which had trained Special Educators. While she was lagging behind mentally, her speech too was not clear enough. Priti had the toughest task of attending to the primary duties of a growing handicapped girl who was now 10 yrs old while her elder sister was 16 yrs of age, who by force of circumstances coupled with her own inherent nature, was extremely ill-behaved towards her. This could be attributed to a multitude of reasons, as explained later in the book. Kiran was oblivious of having lost out on a complete childhood and was growing up, attending a special school which she took a liking to. Her remaining world comprised of his parents and sister and whatever interaction with the outside world by way of parties/ movies or dining out which was seldom.

Hence, quite predominantly she was busy learning from TV serials as it was practically not possible for the parents or the sister to be be with her all the time. Moreover, Mahesh, strongly felt that her perception of human relationships would only progress, watching Tv serials of all kinds representing a communicating medium which had vastly developed over the years.

The readers may find this mundane but it is relevant to point out that such circumstances are encountered and identifiable with millions of people whose mind would tick and efforts can be made on evolving a methodology for leading more harmonious lives through parental introspection and genuine efforts to improve relationship with modern-day youngsters, as has been brought out later in the book

This can only be possible after narrating the actual circumstances as they manifested themselves over the years.

Chapter 4

The Family's first trip to Goa

It was vacation time. The usual summer holidays had started and the family was looking forward to their first trip to Goa in the latter part of June. The mood in the house was that of excitement as Shagun was particularly keen on going there because of the beaches there and the laid-back lifestyle there. So, dates had to be finalised apart from air bookings as well as the hotel.

Some friends had recommended to them to stay in the Northern part of Goa which was considered to be more happening with lively beaches and eating joints.

Seeing the unusual positivity in the atmosphere, Kiran too was upbeat and was busy accumulating her things ranging from colour pencils, drawing books though she was not particularly fond of drawing. It was a result of excitement. She had decided to keep her mobile phone and charger nearly 15 days before the actual date of travel.

It was therefore necessary to explain to her that they were not leaving the next day and it was after a great deal of persuasion that she understood that she could do her packing at a later stage after all the reservations were complete.

Mahesh, was planning to get the reservations done after the mid of june when it was said to intermittently start raining there, making the weather more comfortable.

June is actually off-season time in Goa as the real action is in the months of Dec-January, every year. However, there is an equally heavy rush in june because of the weather as well as the atrractive off season discounts one can get from well known hotels there.

Mahesh managed to strike a good bargain and a package was worked for a period of ten days comprising of two rooms, inter-connected, so that Kiran does not feel isolated as she was used to going to her parents' room in the house before finally sleeping and once during the night as well. Moreover, Priti was used to this part of her duties and always used to ensure that the hotel they stayed in, at any location, should be in a position to offer interconnectivity in rooms.

Hence, she too was thrilled to get this confirmation from Mahesh. Shagun was happy too as she had an independent room and had no qualms about sharing it with Kiran. So, for once it was a happy family looking forward to their first ever visit to a much sought after location in India ie Goa.

Finally, it was time to pack and go the very next day. Kiran, to start with, packed her charger and a huge no of hankys which she dotes on while Shagun packed her laptop and charger apart from her clothes with her objective of doing a lot of streetside shopping. She had already excitedly informed her parents well in advance, that apart from visiting beaches she was going to do a lot of shopping. Priti was busy packing clothes for Mahesh, Kiran and her own self as well as other necessities required there.

Mahesh, came late from office the day before leaving for Goa, coordinating several things required to be taken care of, in his absence. On returning to the house, he straightaway kept all his credit cards as well as money and checked his medicines as well as those which were required for the family.

It was a well timed flight and the family was required to reach the delhi airport at 10 am. Both Mahesh and Priti woke up well in time, while Kiran excitedly got up too. Shagun as usual, was always a late riser and had to be persisted with to finally be able to wake up. Priti had to finally raise her voice to jerk her up.

In the process, Shagun yelled at her spoiling the holiday mood before departing. Mahesh intervened to explain to Shagun that it was getting late and she needed to get up immediately. Invariably, Shagun, by force of habit used to shout everyday in the morning as she was used to sleeping late.

In earlier years, our parents used to emphasise the need to sleep on time and get up early in the morning to start the day whether it was on account of studies or even starting the day afresh.

However, the youngsters of today sleep late, busy socialising on Facebook and a variety of other means of communication through the net. These mediums have developed as social networking mediums of interacting, changing the entire definition of communication.

Hence, for students and those who are free-lancing like Shagun faced a herculean task of getting up early in the morning. Both Mahesh and Priti along with Kiran used to ensure that Shagun was not perturbed in the morning in normal circumstances. However, there was no option now as they had to reach the airport in time to be able to catch the flight to Goa. So, finally she got up to freshen up and leave for the airport.

The morning dust settled and the family left for the airport, in an excited mode, realising that they were visiting Goa for the first time. Post-check in, Shagun was busy looking up things in the shops while Priti was quick to get breakfast for the family. Kiran was very excited primarily because her sister alongwith her parents, a rare feature, were accompanying her.

It was time to board the flight. There were snacks available on board the aircraft, on payment. The plane landed at the airport amidst drizzling rain. And there was a gentle breeze as well. The weather was beautiful though humid. The car mahesh had arranged was airconditioned and it was a privilege to witness different looking residential quarters lined on the way apart from the green surroundings. It was a beautiful sight.

Shagun was excitedly showing various locations on the way apart from clicking photographs on the way. The journey from the airport to the hotel was about 1 1/2 hrs away and the family was enjoying every bit of the journey. The spiralling roads in one part of the route were in the midst of dense greenery and presented a beautiful sight, the family finally reached the hotel with 5 star amenities and the lobby at the entrance of the hotel presented a breathtaking view of the beach ahead. They were quickly escorted to the rooms which were on the ground floor and as requested, were interconnected. The rooms were plush with all facilities and an adjoining balcony with each room.

The view of the greenery all around and the beach ahead, was a vintage sight. Kiran was thrilled more because she saw her parents as well as her sister in an elated frame of mind. Rarely, had she seen her family so happy. In the process she planted a couple of kisses on the cheeks of both Mahesh and Priti. Mahesh had tears in his eyes on seeing this, as a happy and harmonious atmosphere was missing in their house on a routine basis. Priti, too, was tearful and gave an all-understanding look to Mahesh. Shagun was looking around and came in and said "Papa and mom, thank you for this trip" In response, Mahesh said "You are most welcome"

Shagun smiled and went to her room, maybe because she found the situation a trifle embarassing and awkward as this atmosphere was something which the members of the family were not accustomed to, on a routine basis.

It required a holiday to actually purchase happiness. It was time to have lunch and the family chose to have it in the hotel, and look up the various amenities in and around the hotel. Post lunch, the parents and Kiran decided to rest while Shagun decided to go and visit the hotel's private beach and spent some time there in front of the lashing waves. The beach was neat and clean and properly mantained by the hotel.

In the evening, Mahesh deciced to visit the gym to do some brisk walking on the treadmill, while Priti was busy unpacking. Kiran chose to watch tv while Shagun was chatting with her friends. The family then went for a stroll in the sprawling premises of the hotel as well as sat in the lobby for a while. The ambience of the hotel was admirable and it was a treat to look up their various restaurants within the hotel.

Later on, the family returned to the rooms and Mahesh had a drink while Priti sipped some white wine. In fact, Shagun, expressed a desire to have a glass of wine as well, while Kiran too had a couple of sips. It was holiday time! The family was in a buoyant mood and were thoroughly enjoying themselves.

Early next morning, it had started raining heavily and the outside view from the balconies was an artist's paradise. The breakfast was included in the room tariff and there was a sumptuous array of delicacies. There was bacon and eggs to combine with, apart from different varieties if cheese and salads. There were Goan dishes as also south Indian dishes and the entire spread was a delight. The family returned to the rooms to get ready and decide the course of action for the day.

Priti and Mahesh were both keen to visit another beach in Northern Goa which was reported to be lively with adjoining sought after eating joints. Shagun, on the other hand was keen on going out for shopping. There was instant discord as Priti tried hard to explain to her that they were there for a good nine days more and she could shop the very next day. However, Shagun had decided to shop only and at this rigidity, Mahesh lost his cool and fired her, trying to make her realise that she was a grown up and could no longer be so childish.

In response, Shagun announced that she would stay in the hotel and would not go anywhere. The festive atmosphere suddenly took a jolt. Kiran, realising the gravity of the situation, looked sad and downtrodden. She was used to this atmosphere in the house on a daily basis, and could do little to avoid it. Her special mind, however, did not accept this and she approached her sister, imploring her to come along to the beach, in broken language with limited vocabulary, but managed to evoke a reaction from Shagun, who told her to go away as she was in huff, as she had been just fired by her father.

They all got ready and Priti went up to Shagun to tell her that they would first shop for her and then go the beach. Shagun finally agreed and the family decided to to go to that part of Goa which was well known for different varieties of clothes for youngsters specifically. At the sight of the shops, Shagun emitted a cry of delight, and so did Kiran, in a show of solidarity with her sister. Priti, gave an all encompassing smile to Mahesh who instantly understood that he should behave himself and be his usual self.

The next three hours were spent in the market, something which was not Mahesh's idea of fun as he was not overly fond of shopping. He used to enter one shop and take a decision rather than going from one shop to another to finally take a decision. Hence, Kiran and Mahesh had to be content with sitting on steps leading to the shops.

It was now Shagun who took initiative to mend fences with her father and decided to show some dresses to him which she proposed to buy. Mahesh, applied self-restraint and looked at all the dresses one by one, appreciating them and commending her choice. Priti, glanced at him, nodding in approval. Finally, shopping spree ended with Shagun thoroughly satisfied, and the family then proceeded to Calungate beach. What a sight it was! An eating joint adjacent to the beach, full of fun-loving people busy eating and drinking.

On the morning of the next day, ie the third day, it 9am in the morning and Kiran was desperately trying to wake up Priti. "Mom, get up we have to go for breakfast and then go somewhere!" Little did she know that her parents were awake till 3am in the morning, talking to each other regarding family matters. Priti woke up, hugged her and enquired whether Shagun was awake or not Kiran replied in her broken but meaningful English "she is sleeping but also not sleeping as she is busy listening to music with headphones on"

Priti got up and saw that Mahesh, too, was in deep slumber. She cozied up to him and whispered that it was time for breakfast. Kiran planted a kiss on her father's cheek, saying "Papa, get up immediately!" The effect was spontaneous. He got up and went to the other room. He politely said "Shagun, get up, we have to go for breakfast!" Prompt came the reply! "Go to hell and don't bother me"

Exercising self restraint on the lines of what was being discussed in the previous night, Mahesh walked away. Priti had just come out of the wash room and tried to wake up Shagun. In, response, she replied "You do not have any manners, go away" Priti while losing it replied "You are worsening day by day and have no respect left for your parents!" Shagun retorted "I am what I am, I will not have any breakfast today" Kiran, seeing this reacted "Shagun, you are an ill mannered fool, rot here!"

The three of them without Shagun decided to proceed for breakfast. The unprovoked outburst from Shagun would leave any parent enraged. It requires an immense amount of self control to digest this kind of irrational behaviour from a daughter. Here she was on a holiday, shopping the way she wanted to taking everything for granted. Unlike the previous day, the trio had their breakfast though not happily, after Shagun's mis-behaviour. Priti mentioned "I should not have lost my balance, maybe then she would have come too, as we are all on a holiday."

Mahesh responded "she is a grown up girl and, in return for everything that is being done for her, the least she could do is to behave herself!" Priti replied "Then, what is the difference between us and her?" Mahesh kept quiet realising that what Priti was saying was correct. Shagun has to see the difference in us to be able to change herself. With the breakfast over, the trio went and sat in the lobby for some time, staring at the sea ahead, hoping for a sense of positivity in the atmosphere. A little later, they returned to the rooms. Much to their surprise and astonishment, they saw Shagun munching her breakfast and watching TV. Mahesh thought that Shagun had smartly managed to tell the waiter to get the breakfast from the buffet in the restaurant and conveniently have it in the room.

He did not say anything and sat down on the sofa to watch TV too. As soon as he done so, the bell rang and the waiter was there with the bill. He was dazed to see that the bill pertained to breakfast which Shagun had ordered, which was otherwise included in the room tariff. Hence, she conveniently ordered breakfast for herself, without any concern for the fact that her father would have to pay for it something that was entirely avoidable, as it was complementary and therefore, free of cost. It was a gross wastage of money.

Mahesh decided to confront Shagun on this. He said "You could have come along for breakfast and this payment could have been avoided." Characteristically, Shagun retorted "If you can argue on such a trivial things, let me foot the bill as I am also earning and can afford to pay such payments." Mahesh got enraged at this and said "What you deserve are two slaps across the face. You have lost your common sense or thrown it somewhere. If you have to behave like this do not come with us in future" Shagun's reaction at this was even more atrocious!

She said "Ok, if that is the case, I will take the next flight home" Mahesh had completely lost his level of tolerance and retorted "If that is the case, pl pay for it also." Shagun replied "Fine, I will do so" Kiran, on hearing this, started crying. Priti was nonplussed! And did not know how to react. It was Kiran who went scampering after her sister, requesting her not to go. "What will I do?" was her question. Mahesh went and sat in the balcony.

Shagun had already started packing. Priti, the mother knew that her elder daughter was fully capable to take off on her own. She approached Mahesh with an enquiring look and said "Sort it out". A little later, Shagun came and announced "I am not going due to Kiran, she needs me to be with her." Mahesh and Priti actually heaved a sigh of relief. Kiran was all smiles and suddenly the atmosphere was not as pessimistic as earlier.

This was one of the innumerous instances of similar situations which used to develop suddenly throwing all efforts at sorting out their relationship with Shagun, out of gear. Earlier, when Shagun was younger, both Mahesh and Priti tried their level best to counsel her and try to explain to her in every conceiveable way to improve her basic understanding of different situations. As parents, they tried to convey to her that whatever they suggest and do would be in her best interest.

However, the situation went from bad to worse and became even more complicated over time. Sometimes, Mahesh and Priti used to wonder as to what they needed to do to improve this situation. Both also felt that they were required to exercise greater self control and not react impulsively in any interaction with Shagun. Moreover, the parents are also reqd to figure out, what else are they required to do to mend fences with their children.

The family of four got ready and were all set to and visit church in Goa as also take a cruise on the Panjim Sea. The mood became buoyant once again and finally it was time to board the ship for a cruise with blaring music on. The view from the ship was a treat to watch and the staff of the ship did a stage show and everybody joined in for dancing to the beat. This was followed by snacks and varieties of soft and hard drinks. It was a great deal of fun by the time the cruise was over it was 5pm in the evening.

Instead of going to the hotel, the family decided to go to Panjim market to look around. The market bore a cosmopolitan look. There was a variety of branded shops with clothes for men and women. Shagun was excited and disappeared inside one of them. Priti was busy looking up for herself as well as Kiran. Mahesh did not see any sense in buying normal clothes which are available. The shopping, two days back was from another market and were typically of the go an variety. The family had done quite a bit of purchasing that day. Here they were again all set of blowing up more money.

He asked Priti "What is the point of buying these garments which are available in all these shops in a no of malls all over the city of Delhi.?" Priti replied "We do not go so frequently to these malls in Delhi. Here there is ample time at our disposal, and you, the financier is also around" So, Mahesh had no option but to wait for the ladies to take their own time in shopping. Soon thereafter, Shagun came rushing out to call Priti to have a look at the clothes she had selected. Mahesh was aghast at the bill which was around Rs 10,000 /-.

On one hand is her extremely discourteous behaviour which, at this point of time, she had forgotten completely and here was she buying an expensive array of fashion garments. Mahesh, decided to convey his thoughts to Priti. She responded "What is the option?" Mahesh was perplexed at this reply from Priti. Children cannot take their parents for granted when it comes to their needs and have no control on their behaviour towards them. How else would they ever realise?. He chose to tell Shagun "This is turning out to be an expensive holiday! You have shopped to your satisfaction two days back, and again.! What will I get in return?"

Shagun remarked "What do you want?" By now Kiran had got serious also. Priti had also got rather circumspect. Shagun smirked and replied "If you cannot let us shop, why did you have children in the first place?" Mahesh was nonplussed! He paid the bill and decided to avoid creating a scene at the shop. This time he was determined not to spoil the holiday mood and with some degree of difficulty managed to keep a control on his reactions. However, he was decided to enter into a discussion with Shagun after talking to Priti, in Goa itself.

They got back to the hotel and decided to relax in their rooms. Mahesh chose to read a while and Priti as well as Kiran took a quick nap. Shagun was busy having a relook at all her purchases and could be seen grinning to herself.

Mahesh was in the process of reading a book on Swami Vivekananda's teachings, which coincidentally talked about how it is so necessary to shed anger, ego, arrogance and hold our own selves for all that is happening with us and not hold anyone else responsible for our agonies. In short, it meant that we are able to change our circumstances through "Self change."

We all have varying degrees of anger, ego, arrogance irritability, sulking as well as begrudging our existence, at different points of time when we are in a negative frame of mind. An improvement in these negative traits would definitely have a positive impact on our external environment.

Mahesh was strongly impacted by these concepts and was faltering in the application in day-to-day life. In the context of his own family, Priti too was very clearheaded in this regard but had a problem in controlling her impulses when it came to her interaction with Shagun.

It was 9pm and Mahesh and Priti did not feel like eating anything heavy on the tummy. Shagun, by now had fallen asleep. So Priti checked with Kiran who had just got up from her nap and ordered just soup and sandwhiches for themselves. Priti spoke to Mahesh "Are you ok?" Mahesh replied "I am fine but we must talk to her as to why she is behaving like this specially when everything is being done for her"

Priti responded "The effect of whatever is done for Shagun goes away if you show it as an obligation. She is 18 yrs of age and will not be able to digest her father constantly reminding her of this reality. It is not a give and take relationship!" Mahesh was surprised and said "This thought of what we are doing for our children comes only when they misbehave with us. As parents it is our duty, but that also does not mean that we cannot expect minimum regard and respect from them. Are we asking for too much?"

Priti looked bewildered. Mahesh continued "Do not feel pressurised! This is not a problem that only we are encountering! It must be a common problem in all households. We need to also sort it out as this was affecting Kiran and her special mindset. We cannot allow this as she would develop distorted views of human relationships."

It was 11pm and both Mahesh and Priti decided to end this conversation there and continue later on. It was the fifth day in Goa. The three ladies decided to go for a swim. Mahesh chose to hit the gym, as there was a lot of eating and drinking going on for the last couple of days, since they arrived in Goa. As they had got up early, the family was ready for breakfast very unlike the previous day, when the fracas had taken place. It started raining heavily soon thereafter and continued for three hours ruling out the possibility of going anywhere in the prelunch session.

While Shagun got busy with her laptop, Kiran was busy making sketches in her drawing book.

Mahesh, sitting in the balcony, with Priti decided to continue where he had left the previous night. He resumed "So, Priti, did you enjoy your stay in Goa so far?" Priti replied "Yes certainly, barring these skirmishes which keep taking place with Shagun, I guess we cannot have best of all the worlds. This is perhaps a part of our karma which we can continue fighting." Mahesh remarked "I agree. But, we must win also. We need to keep moving forward and take action for the same. Merely sulking will not help"

In came Shagun in the room's balcony. "So, I am your problem child. Does it ever occur to you as to where are you both are going wrong. It is very easy for you to point fingers at me." Mahesh smiled "Ok, the weather is beautiful, pl tell us about our follies"

Shagun smirked and replied "Papa, you have a bad habit of making me constantly realise what you both have done for me in the past. It is very annoying!" Mahesh replied "All that you are expected to do is to show basic minimum regard and respect for your parents, which you do not do. I can cite several instances when you have acted irrationally, devoid of any sense of logic or reasoning. In fact, there have been innumerous such occurences!

When you behave like this, we are reminded of what all we are doing for you, something which is entirely avoidable, as you are our daughter. You must understand that there was no need to for example, to shop to such an extent specially when you are regularly relenishing your wardrobe in Delhi itself. It amounts to an exorbitant expenditure. Your behaviour at breakfast time the other day was most inexplicable." Shagun replied "You chose to also say that you will slap me hard. Is that the way to talk to an 18 yr old girl?."

Mahesh responded "I admit I should not have said this, will you also like to acknowledge your mistakes. Lets both improve ourselves" Priti also chipped in "Parents will always think well for their children but the chidren should also learn to respect their parents. Look at your way of talking to both of us, is this what we expect from you?" Shagun, at this simply shrugged her shoulders and walked away.

It was a very casual response to what her parents had to say. Mahesh's parents are today not around but it was simply inconceiveable for him to disrespect his parents in any circumstance. The same could be said for Priti.

The generation gap as we all understand reflects the difference in mindsets of different age groups of people. In earlier days, particularly in countries like India women were more identified with household work and not working in offices. It was predetermined that post-marriage women would look after the house as well as bring up their children. Hence, any strategic decision making did not involve the opinion of women.

With the passage of time women have increasingly become career oriented, in view of ever escalating inflation when it has become necessary not to additional of sources of income.

Hence, a new era started when both husband and wife started working in regular jobs. But the mindsets did not change! The husband still nursed all expectations from the wife despite the fact that she was also doing a regular job. Similarly, the son's parents also wanted that their daughter-in law fulfilled their expectations as well.

Times changed further when the women started realising that it was humanly impossible for them to lead a life when they were required to earn as well as look after the in-laws also. Moreover, unlike earlier times women felt more in this new mould where they found themselves financially independent. Their importance in their married family also grew.

This sense of newly acquired independence has already started affecting young girls like Shagun who are rightly career minded like millions of others but fail to realise that they would still have a lot of adjustment to do even though they may be earning independently. Even today, it is the girls who leave their houses and get married and adjust in the husband's family. This lack of maturity in the minds of young girls later on creates disharmony in their married lives.

It was this apprehension in the minds of both Mahesh and Priti which seemed to keep growing as Shagun was yet to be able to adjust to her own parents. It therefore logically followed that Shagun must pursue her career oriented dreams but not at the cost of a harmonious married life. The concept of nuclear families has taken roots in the minds of youngsters wherein they do not have in-laws to contend with and have to manage their spouse only, to start with and then their own children, later on. The knack of adjusting to a given environment should be inculcated by young girls much before they start their married life.

Back in Goa the rain had stopped and the family was in the process of readying themselves to go out. Mahesh was keen on seeing a movie, an idea to which Priti readily agreed but Shagun was more keen to go and visit the southern part of Goa. The family had to follow what Shagun had suggested and it was a picturesque drive amidst greenery on either side of the road.

On reaching there, it gave the look of a cluster of several five star hotels and various hotels with lesser ratings. There was a restaurant namely "fisherman's wharf" on the side of river flowing there. It was around 4pm and they decided to have tea with some seafood as snacks. Shagun got busy clicking photographs, as it was a beautiful sight. Kiran was feeling sleepy and was all set for an after noon nap. They visited another five star hotel and were delighted to see the anbience there. They decided to then go to movie theatre and saw a Hindi movie which turned out to be interesting. Kiran had already slept on the way and was happily clapping at times in the movie, much to the agony others sitting there who were getting disturbed. It was 930pm when it ended and they decided to have a bite on the way before reaching the hotel. They stopped at hotel overlooking Panjim Sea and had their dinner

The family had three days left to further enjoy there. Mahesh and Priti decided to visit the beach every day, and specially Calungut Beach where they had a wonderful time in the first couple of days. Hence, the very next day, they visited the same beach and this time tried several of their dishes as well as the desserts. Mahesh had a couple of glasses of white wine while Shagun and Priti had one each. Then they spent some time at the beach. It was an amazing experience! Finally when they were about to go,

Shagun requestingly said "Papa can we go for one last time to shop?" Mahesh was simply dumbounded.!

After all the interaction the previous day, Shagun was back to square one. She wanted to shop and had the audacity to mention this to her papa who had reprimanded her for excessive shopping. Kiran, despite being a special child, with her impaired speech managed to say to her sister "Are you mad?" Shagun lost it and in front of everybody slapped her. "Kiran, don't you dare talk to me like this!" She then walked to the car.

Priti, then, quickly followed her and pulled her car, "How did have the cheek to hit your sister, knowing that she has drawbacks, of a special nature." "You are a disgusting daughter!" Prompt was Shagun's response "You too, mother, like father like mother" Priti was simply amazed at Shagun's brazenness. They all sat in the car and proceeded to the hotel. Kiran was all tears & started pinching her sister. Priti immediately checked her.

There was an eerie silence in the car after a hearty meal and a good time at the beach. It was a pity that in their family the situation changes from moment to moment. Such is the transition from a happy state to a state to an atmosphere that is abruptly dismal, that it almost gave the impression that it was the force of karma, which was in play, the situation had worsened over time and had become irreversible.

There were times when both Mahesh and Priti wondered what was in store for Kiran if they were not around, as Shagun's preoccupations would increase over time and post-marriage, even more.

Despite the strong bonding which undoubtedly existed between Shagun and Kiran, it was primarily not Shagun's responsibility to take care of Kiran for all times to come. At this juncture, Kiran had not shown any specific interest in any area which could be considered for her as an occupation. Though Mahesh at times used to confidently mention that Kiran could always get absorbed in his office, he always had a lingering doubt whether that, as a daily routine would sustain Kiran's interest or not. Priti, as a mother used to try hard to ascertain whether cooking was of interest to Kiran or not, but so far both had failed to pinpoint where her interest lies.

The holiday planned for Goa, as earlier, was a mixed experience. It was exhilarating a times and hit an unexplainable low on other occasions. Nevertheless, it was definitely a change from the dreary routine back in Delhi. However, it was a stark reality that holidays should spur you on to make your routine comfortable and sustainable. In the case of this family, cohesiveness was missing and their was no rapport between the parents and the elder daughter, Shagun.

It was the penultimate day in Goa and all the four were busy packing for their return to Delhi. There was hardly any communication between the parents and Shagun. Kiran, was hesitatingly, approaching her to revive communication channels and did manage to get a positive response. A little later both were seen playing cards. Obviously, Shagun realised that it was not correct on her part to have slapped Kiran the previous day.

The next day the focus was on leaving the hotel on time to board the flight back home. There was minimal communication between the parents and Shagun. All the positives in terms of excessive shopping which was in the previous days had got nullified due to bitter interactions from time to time, between parents and Shagun.

Finally it was time to board the flight back to Delhi and the sporadically troubled family reached Delhi safely, and found their house all set to welcome them to the rigours of the daily routine.

Chapter 5

Predicament of a Mother—
a Housemaker and the Focal Point

A unique combination of a wife, mother, daughter-in-law all rolled into one is this one lady and the focal point in every house hold ie Priti in the instant storyline. Priti came from a highly cultured family with her father being a senior bureaucrat with a vast set of connections in terms of friends and relatives

It was a longtime back that the two families had met as also the boy ie Mahesh and Priti who had met initially and gave their respective consents to their parents and entered into a life long commitment to each other ie marriage. Mahesh was self employed and was earning comfortably well. Priti had been brought up with all the training which her mother could have imparted to her so as to facilitate a comfortable married life for Priti. In the first decade of marriage,

Priti had to contend with the vagaries and expectations af Mahesh's parents, but had the satisfaction of the support of her husband, Mahesh. Moreover, Priti had the onerous responsibility of looking after a handicapped younger daughter as well a school-going elder daughter. The collective task cut out for her was burdensome and Mahesh tried to give his wholehearted support to her.

Mahesh did understand her predicament and realised that it was not easy for her to strike a balance in all her duties. Priti used to cry at times, looking at Kiran and future as well as the larger-than-life expectations of her in-laws. Therefore, Mahesh, used to ensure that they did intermittently go out for a movie or have dinner outside, ta provide a change to his wife as well as spend some time with her.

Priti at times used to say "Mahesh, without your undivided support it would not have been possible for me to cope up with all my responsibilities." Pat came the reply in a lighter vein "Sweetheart, you struck gold in marrying me. I will never let you down" Ten years had gone by and the bonding was as strong as ever. Priti used to say "Shagun dotes on Kiran and we are lucky that they are developing a strong emotional bond as time passes."

A recap . . . .

Both Shagun and Mahesh did not realise that Shagun who was 6 yrs of age when Kiran was born, also required time to be devoted to her. She was used to their total attention before Kiran's birth. In fact, relatives and friends used to always express their disbelief at Shagun's ability to socialise so easily with all age groups of people. Her perpetual smile at even passersby was also reciprocated by all and sundry. Shagun, quite frequently, used to approach her mother to play with her as in earlier days, prior to Kiran's birth. "Mom, can we play "Cooking in kitchen", (a popular kids game)?" mom replied "Shagun can't you see that I am busy with Kiran?" Shagun walked away grumbling.

Likewise, she asked Mahesh he after he got back one day "Papa, can we play a game of Ludo (kids game)?" Papa retorted back "I have just got back from office, I am tired" Shagun replied "Then, whom do I play with?" Mahesh busy with thoughts concerning office, said "Do not get after me, go talk to your mother!" Shagun at the age of 5-6 yrs was too small to react any further as she started doing in later years. She simply walked away

This is one such example when Mahesh as a parent should have reacted sensibly instead of shooing Shagun away. Parents cannot take refuge under the pressure related to office or house, as it is their direct responsibility to take care of their children they have brought into this world. It is invariably seen that parents look forward to having children conceptually, but fail to do justice when it comes to applying themselves in daily life.

That day Mahesh was in a bad mood due to work pressure and told Priti "I have just got back, can you not engage Shagun in something?" Shagun responded "Look, I am busy, too with Kiran! Can't you see?" Mahesh lost it and reacted "There is no peace in the house as well" Priti retorted "If that is the case, do not come back and stay in office" Mahesh howled "Shut up and get lost!"

Priti started crying while a six year old Shagun watched in silence, and the poor toddler, Kiran, gaping at her weeping mother. A commonly seen and heard of incident in daily lives of millions of couples, but most undesirable!

Priti and Mahesh were in the process of growing in their marriage in terms of mutual understanding and maturity. The children were small and demanding. Ideally, the parents should be enjoying this friendly task of taking care of the kids and their kiddish requirements.

However, it is widely seen that parents are under pressure in terms of financial needs which keep growing in this modern day world where relative comparisons are a rule of the day. Therefore, the stature of the school the children are going to, the kind and number of cars owned, the type of accomodation being lived in, and the brand of clothes worn on routine basis, are some examples which trigger off a relative analysis of the networth of a family.

The society has undergone a radical shift particularly in countries like India. This is evident from this instance given in this chapter. Shagun was ten years of age and her birthday was fast approaching. She inquired from her mother "Mummy, can we celebrate my birthday in a five star hotel?" Priti was understandably taken aback! She asked "It will be greater fun in the house and I will cook a variety of dishes and sweets!.."

Prompt came the reply "Varsha, my friend is also planning to celebrate her birthday in a five star hotel, I want to be one-up on her and do so before her. There are children in my class who have done so in the past." Priti finally told her "Sweetheart, we cannot celebrate in a hotel, that too, a five star hotel, as it will cost a lot of money" Shagun's mind was working at breakneck speed and said "You have two cars and can't afford to celebrate my birthday in a hotel that means that you do not love me."

Priti was at a loss of words at this reaction of Shagun, and said "We love you very much. We will get you a good gift. What do you want?" Shagun was shrewd negotiator and said "A laptop" Priti was again taken for a surprise! She had not heard of any ten year old boy or girl owning a laptop.

She said "You have to concentrate on your studies and also take classes for tuitons in a few subjects. There will be no time for you to use the laptop." "I am right! You don't love me anymore, you only love Kiran. You are busy with her all the time. You do not play with me anymore." Priti was defeated! She replied "Lets talk it over with papa when he comes back from office." The communication had reached a point when it was impossible to convince Shagun, to the contrary.

Shagun was smart enough to bring up the issue at dinner time, when her papa was also there. On hearing what she had to say, as narrated above, Mahesh looked dazed and directed his gaze at Priti, almost accusing her of Shagun's unreasonable request. Priti merely shrugged her shoulders!

Mahesh was more direct and said "Sweetheart, that is not possible! Neither can we spend in a five star hotel nor can we buy you a laptop. We will buy you a good gift, which you want apart from this." Shagun started crying and got up and walked away from the dining table. Priti went scampering after her.

Kiran too, sported a serious look at this juncture! Later on, before retiring for the day, Mahesh asked Priti "What happened?" Priti instantly understood what he wanted to know. And said "Times have changed drastically! Look at what she is learning in the school. If this is what she wants now, do you realise what is in store for us in the future. You cant blame her friends either! There are schools today which are fully airconditioned. If this is how children are going to grow then their capacity to tolerate and persevere would be drastically low!"

Mahesh readily agreed. He said "I know but what do we do? She is yet to mature! Moreover, if this is on her mind then what values would she nurture in times to come. As it is, she is upset as we do not have time to play with her, or devote to her. Let us try our level best."

Recap . . . . (continued)

Kiran, on the other hand had barely started to walk, at an age when small children are commonly seen to run all around the house. It was a clear indication of things to come. As she was lagging behind mentally, every aspect of her upbringing would accordingly be equally delayed. Priti had to toughen herself for difficult times to come. Mahesh, too, started realising that without his explicit moral support it would be very difficult for her to cope up with handling the primary duties of growing girl until she is an adult, hoping that she would in her growing years be able to becoming less dependent on her mother for primary duties.

Mahesh also realised the frequent need to have a change in the form of seeing a movie or dining out. Kiran had started going to special school which was equipped with special educators. Kiran used to enjoy going to school as she got an opportunity to mingle around with other special children.

Priti was discussing these matters on one day with Mahesh who responded "I know it is not easy for you to manage Kiran and the fast growing Shagun. I hardly have any role to play, as I am preoccupied with office which is quite demanding. We will also have to keep a tab on the traits which Shagun is inculcating as time passes." Priti replied "Shagun is slowly and gradually developing an antagonistic attitude towards both of us and is increasingly impacted by her school friends."

"Why is this so" asked Mahesh. Priti said "Look, when she regularly sees me busy with Kiran and you in office, she will automatically drawn towards friends. Moreover, she is nearing 12 yrs and is growing fast. She is now not cribbing about our lack of involvement with her. This is what is worrying me because I do not want her to grow to become a self-centred person without any consideration for family values." Mahesh said "We must talk to her as lack of communication could worsen the situation."

The following day was a Sunday and Mahesh and Priti decided to stay indoors and spend some quality time with

Shagun as well. They decided to talk to her, post breakfast. However, they were in for a shock when they decided to talk to her. "I am busy now and later my friend is coming home." Priti said "Ok, when you are free we would like to talk to you. Just let know."

Mahesh resisted the urge to shout at Shagun for this response of her's. She realised that the situation is undoubtedly getting out of hand. He decided to wait for Shagun to get free from her friend and then meet her. Priti too, was taken aback. She had an inkling that things vis-à-vis Shagun were not shaping very well.

The two waited anxiously for Shagun to come to them after her friend had gone away, but that did not happen. It was 7pm and they decided to once again go to her room. This time it was Mahesh who took the initiative to start the communication.

He started off "Are you upset with us?. Pl understand that you are as close to our heart as Kiran. You know that Kiran needs help in everything and that is why your mom is not able to spend so much time with you as before. Even I have got busier than before in office."

Shagun responded "So, what can I do? Don't worry I have grown up and have friends to spend time with rather than listen to lectures from both of you." Priti responded "Is this the way to talk to your father?" Shagun retaliated "I do not want to talk to you either." It was now Mahesh's turn to give her a piece of his mind regarding her behaviour. "Are you out of your mind? Is this the way to talk to your parents?"

Shagun replied "You both take care of your office and house, let me take care of myself" it dawned upon the parents that Shagun had been irreversibly affected by the fact that Mahesh was busier in office while Priti was more occupied in attending to Kiran's needs, after her birth. However, Shagun was developing a close bond with Kiran as was evident from the time she was spending with her. This was a huge plus! Times were changing rapidly and so were the mindsets of young children as well as their level of awareness and maturity. Both Mahesh and Priti decided to take the children out for dinner, in the middle of the week.

So, the following Wednesday, Mahesh came home early and told Shagun "Lets go and have dinner in some good restaurant!" Shagun for once had a broad smile on her face. The parents were relieved! Shagun remarked "Mummy does not make anything tasty, I am fed up. Lets go and have Chinese food" Mahesh said "So, now you do not like anything mom makes! You used to be so happy till a few months back." Shagun replied "Mummy, is all the time busy with Kiran, she has forgotten how to make food."

Priti was shellshocked on hearing this as she used to make it a point to ask Shagun everyday a meal or tiffin had to be cooked. She almost felt like crying and walked away. Mahesh new that the problem was not food, but Shagun's attitude. Priti was well known amongst relatives and friends for her cooking skills and that, too, all types ie Indian, continental, Chinese and various types of other snacky foods as well. In fact, Mahesh was nursing a desire of opening a take away eating joint, keeping in mind Priti's cooking skills.

Nevertheless, the family went out for dinner to a popular restaurant, mainly to please Shagun. They were otherwise keen on having continental food, anyways. They ordered different varieties with the intention of consuming the leftovers next day at home. Shagun, however, did not find anything tasty, had soup and a dessert and was over with her dinner. Yet again, the parents were taken aback.

This was her favourite place! What had happened? The preceding 1-2 years seem to have changed everything. Shagun said "Rotten food! Noodles are bad! I cant have it!" Priti remarked "This is your favourite place. What has changed here?" Shagun replied "Both you and this place are no longer the same!" Mahesh looked helplessly at the situation!

Later at home, Priti spoke to Mahesh "Lets go and meet her teachers! We cannot ignore it! The situation is getting out of hand. I do not see any logic in the way she has suddenly started behaving." Mahesh realising the gravity of the situation, readily agreed. Both of them decided to go to her school on the following Saturday.

The teachers had also started noticing a change in Shagun's mannerisms in the last few months and attributed it to her company of friends. This was now an even more difficult situation. To ward off her friends from Shagun, was an impossible task! She would completely mis-understand her parents for first ignoring her, not spending enough time with her and then victimising her by ensuring a breakup between her and her friends.

Shagun's group of friends had grown in bonding over the previous 2-3years and they had been frequenting each others' places regularly. Priti did, by and large, keep a watch but had no control on what they used to talk about, apart from playing with each other. She had obviously had no clue about her visits to their places. Her friends belonged to rich families and got dropped in chauffeur-driven swanky cars.

It dawned upon her that the parents of her friends were leading a hectic social life with little time left for children. Therefore, perhaps Shagun found solace in their company since her parents were not able to spend time with her due to force of circumstances, largely beyond their control. Since parental preoccupations was a common factor, their bonding strengthened and they became emotionally close to each other, along with a sense of insecurity which was bridged with their friendship.

It was a complex situation and required the parents to meet each other and take steps to ensure that the problem does not persist further. To their surprise and astonishment, the friends' parents were comfortable with the situation and did not find anything amiss. On the contrary, they pulled up Mahesh and Priti for overreacting to the situation.

It is a super fast changing modern day world where the value system had undergone a sea-change. Mahesh and Priti were numbed at the apathy displayed by the parents. They were clueless as to what action to take to mend the messy situation which had developed on the home-front.

They thought and discussed time and again, and came to a mutual consensus that they would become more tolerant towards Shagun and be nice to her in any situation. If the situation warranted parental guidance, the same would be done with love and affection.

What Mahesh and Priti planned was to change themselves to an extent that Shagun started noticing a change in her parents and, in the process, change herself. It was a difficult task, the implementation of which would not be easy. Parents cannot stop discharging their role as parents, and need to keep correcting their wards whenever they were erring in anything and everything concerning their lives. This is a universally acknowledged fact and an integral requirement when it concerns the quality of upbringing of children.

Priti had a major role to play because her involvement with the children was relatively much more as compared to Mahesh. Accordingly, she was consciously interacting with Shagun thoughtfully instead of instinctively, as earlier, this was the dire need of the moment to protect the closeness of the chords within the family, which had become more fragile owing to Shagun's recent reactions. Priti stopped scolding her for anything, unlike earlier, though for correct reasons.

She narrated her observations to Mahesh, and said. "Mahesh, you will have to chip in too, contrary to what we had discussed as I am noticing that Shagun is developing traits which are going to make her a very finicky person. For instance, she is more and more prone to disliking anything and everything cooked in the house, unlike earlier years when she did not nurse any such reservations. She has become very temperamental now.

At the drop of a hat, she leaves her food or does not eat properly even if she has been earlier asked what she wanted. To have. Further, her cupboard is entirely messy, and she is not even doing basic things which she is expected to do." Mahesh was surprised and said

"How will I help in all this, you will have to correct her as her mother." Priti said "I would like to do so but it is becoming increasingly difficult to engage her in a conversation as she either retorts back or walks away. The urge to scold her, seeing her misbehaviour becomes irresistible, or is actually necessary also."

Mahesh also realised that he could not afford to be a silent spectator and adopt the convenient option of letting Priti get over-burdened. He said "Priti as much as I would like to help, it will only worsen the situation, as I would not be so tolerant as you are and would end up firing her up" Priti remarked "That is not fair! You are expecting the world out of me. You have to exercise greater self-control and restrain yourself from any undesirable utterances." Mahesh was intelligently reined-in by Priti.

Priti rightly made him understand his role as a father which most fathers avoid under the guise of work-pressure. Mahesh realised that he could not adopt the easy way out. He decided that he would interact more frequently with her on a daily basis.

Hence, while watching a TV program that evening Mahesh took the initiative and spoke "Shagun, how are things in school? When are your friends dropping in?"

Pat came the reply from the twelve year old "Papa, school is fine, and I am studying hard to do well. Do not worry! Why are you asking about my friends? Is there a problem?" Mahesh remarked "Can I not talk to you? I am just doing casual talk. Is that problematic for you?" Shagun replied "No probs! The manner in which you asked was not correct" Mahesh was surprised at the objectivity of the replies to a father. He promptly corrected her "So, now I have to first rehearse what and how I have to talk to you?" The reply was crisp and abrupt "You are simply pathetic!"

Mahesh now realised what Priti was trying to convey to him. Shagun was slowly and gradually become an ill-behaved stubborn girl, who is becoming self-centred and was developing utter dis-regard for her parents. He also realised that this could not be attributed to her friends but was becoming a part of her own mindset which had wrong pre-conceived notions about family and human values. He also found the choice of the word "pathetic" used for her father quite startling.

Priti was however not surprised at the interaction between father and daughter. She was pained at the direction the small family was heading. Last but not the least, Kiran also was being perceptive enough to realise that all was not normal, but was confused in trying to figure out how to react.

She was caught between her little but strong bond with her elder sister and her parents. In her own way, she used to tell her sister in broken language, to talk properly to her parents. In response, she used to be asked to shut up, which she apparently did not mind in these seven years of her life, so far.

Priti's predicament as explained in this chapter is definitely not an isolated instance and is identifiable with the times of today. The emphasis here is on Priti's compulsions as a mother, as a wife and her desperation to try and improve the home situation even to the extent of bringing out a change in her own self, as she discussed with her husband, who was trying to do the same. The desperation to bring about harmony in the family is evident. Priti also realised that the years to come would entail a battle between the generation of parents on one hand and younger clan represented by the growing daughter, on the other hand. The parental approach was to restore peace and harmony at all costs. Lets now move to Mahesh's world and his state of affairs over the years.

Chapter 6

Mahesh a "A Jack of all trades"

At the time of marriage, Mahesh was working in a company handling commercial work. A couple of years later, his childhood friend, Rajiv, approached him with an irresistible offer of taking on an agency of a well known consumer goods giant with a proven image in the market, at large. Mahesh had acquired skills in finance, procurement, sales, administration in his career so far apart from running a small scale unit for about one year, for his late father's friend.

Hence, Mahesh with his rich experience in all deptts of a company, presented an ideal choice to his friend, Rajiv. Rajiv lacked the experience but had the funds given to him by his father.

Mahesh was attracted to Rajiv's proposal and was all set to join him as an equal partner. He had discussed the proposal in detail with Priti as well who too, supported him in his decision making. They had discussed the possibility of a breakup with the other partner who was none other than his childhood friend. Also, Mahesh and Priti had discussed the possibility of the agency not flourishing. Having analysed all the interrelated aspects, Mahesh decided in year'2000 to join him.

The two set up an office and entered into an agreement with the principals and appointed dealers in Delhi as well as other strategic areas. The objective was to reach out to consumers as much as possible. Hence, Mahesh and Rajiv had formed a firm as distributors with a network of dealers in place. The idea was not to be saddled with stocks at any point of time. They proposed to take financial limits from bankers to facilitate stocking of all varieties of products by their principals.

There was a necessity of repeated interaction with dealers in order to keep them motivated and try to sell as much as possible to maximixe profits. It could be best categorised as a trading operation with low margins of profit and a constant need to have a high turnover, in order to generate a sizeable profit over and above total expenses.

The business flourished well till 2007-2008 when the downturn affected their operation also. The customers started buying selected items only and started looking for cheaper substitutes. Both Mahesh and Rajiv were worried, being saddled with stock. Notwithstanding this, the dealers also started getting desperate with stocks not getting liquidated. It was a torrid time they were facing. The principals showed a great deal of understanding and decided to take back slow moving consumer items to reduce the burden of their distributors as well as their dealers.

It was around this time that things were not too conducive at home as well with Shagun turning truant and Priti busy with Kiran's special needs. Mahesh was too bogged down due the situation in office due to the downturn in the industry, at large.

The readers may observe that it was the force of cicumstances which led to Shagun feeling neglected as the parents were preoccupied with their respective functions. They were undoubtedly morally responsible, but being human, it is difficult to strike a perfect balance between different responsibilities, especially in times of adversity. There was nothing deliberate on the part of the parents however, the situation was such that it had distorted Shagun's mindset.

Mahesh explained one day to Priti "It is a mess we are in! However, the remedial measures and the related decisions are jointly taken despite the fact that Rajiv does not have the requisite expertise to decide on the right course of action." Priti rightly said "Since you are together in the business, you will have to decide collectively."

Mahesh expected the principals to offer different solutions to the problem of stock lying with them as well as the dealers, unsold for quite some time. All they agreed to was to take back the slow moving categories of stock. He told Priti "Rajiv was content with this help extended by the principals, without realising that the otherwise fast moving stock was also not selling at the same pace as before. He is unnecessarily apprehensive about the principals getting upset with us"

Priti responded "Try and nicely explain to him without any panic, he will understand." Mahesh was panicking as they were facing a situation where there was a cash crunch and things were fast approaching a point when they would be defaulting in their payment commitments to their principals.

Mahesh told Priti "These companies with a brand image are very touchy when it comes to payments. Any delay or default can cast aspersions on the credibility of the distributor". Mahesh's partnership firm were distributors. The fight was on! The govt was promising measures for revival of the economy. In this battle, Mahesh quite understandably overlooked his role as a father and could not guage the changing mindset of his elder daughter, Shagun.

While Mahesh had the requisite experience, he was not in exclusive control over this business enterprise. Hence, he was even more apprehensive of failing and it was this lurking fear that preoccupied his mind all the time. He left very little scope for the thought of realising his responsibility as a father, an area which he conveniently left to his wife to manage.

This situation must be rampant in millions of households where the breadwinner is too busy earning for the family and psychologically accepts the situation in its existing mode. Priti, on the other hand had also accepted this arrangement with both not focussing enough on Shagun's upbringing especially, in the age group of 7-15 yrs.

As time passed, the industrial atmosphere also improved and the customers also started feeling that the worst had passed and they could lead their normal lives. This was reflected in the increased sales witnessed by Mahesh's firm as well as their dealers.

Mahesh could now heave a sigh of relief with more stability at office and started nursing a new urge to improve things at home.

Chapter 7

The Changing Times

The past decade has witnessed a sea change in the human value system wherein the focus has shifted to nuclear families from the old conventional joint family setup. In fact, in western countries the approach was more on vocationalisation of education and children, after becoming majors would invariably branch out, from the sheltered living, with their parents, to leading their own independent lives confronting life's problems upfront. and trying to win over them.

They did not have the onerous responsibility of looking after their own parents once they reach old age. Parents in western countries were content to live their lives independently without nursing any expectations from their children to directly shoulder any responsibility in doing so.

On the contrary, in some countries the traditional system and related expectations of the parents continued unabatedly in rural areas, unlike urban areas where parents, in old age, increasingly wanted to lead their own lives till the time it was possible. Not every old couple could afford to move to the select—few old age homes in the countries.

However, the basics have to be in order in an over-populated country like India, there have been increasing instances of elderly couples or single parent, living independently, being targeted by criminals for looting their homes and murdering them in some cases. It is impossible for policing to be so elaborate and secure in the background of the requirements of population of unmanageable proportions.

As mentioned earlier in the book, women are also increasingly inclined to work to earn a living, irrespective of the quality of employment. Prospective grooms also desire working brides to augment their earnings. Priti once mentioned to Mahesh "I wish I was earning also, I could have helped you managing the financial requirements of our family." Mahesh promptly replied "In our case, that was not possible as it was more important for you to take care of Kiran's upbringing, an area where I have had no role to play."

Priti said "I could have worked in a school and managed Kiran as well. She is also going to a special school. I could have used that time better" Mahesh agreed and said "You could have done that but it is also important to have your own space and spend some time on yourself also. Normally, if Kiran had been fine, you would not have been attending to her primary needs after she was 5 yrs of age. Kiran is now 12 yrs old and you are still attending to all her needs. I know you are trying to reduce her dependence on you but it will take a longer time in our situation."

Priti understood. However, she found an increasing number of women in her age group, in fulltime jobs. There were frequent occasions when some of them at different points of time would express their surprise on learning that Priti was a house maker only and was not earning a living, despite knowing her specific cicumstances.

One of them recently remarked "You can leave her in a crech and do your job also. That way you can constructively contribute to the family" Priti was hurt! She shared this instance with Mahesh "Does it mean that my role of a mother of a special girl is not constructive enough?" Mahesh smiled "It is a sign of immaturity on the part of your friend to have said this. What you are doing is far more crucial to the stability of our family!"

The very fact that her friend was so casual about leaving Kiran at a crech irked her, as she required constant attention specially for her primary needs. How could she trust anybody to take care of this aspect? Newspapers had been frequently reporting minors being victimised for sexual and other reasons. The thought of this used to send shudders down the spine of both Mahesh and Priti. Where was the world heading in this era? The newspapers were reporting cases of kidnapping, killings within members of the same family for money?

There were cases of road rage reported frequently! Educated people coming from accomplished families were losing it even if their respective cars just touched each other accidentally! The confrontation could reach any limit! Guns/daggers even sticks/rods were drawn out to resort to mindless acts of impulsive violence, resulting in death for some. Such was the pent up frustration in these cases that it is let out in response to trivial acts of provocation. Life has no meaning! It can be snuffed out within an instant!

Priti narrated one such incident to Mahesh "Here was a case of a gym instructor who when provoked, suddenly sat in his car and ran it over the individual he was arguing with a minute back, regarding the scraping of the two cars on the road amidst heavy traffic.

The man was so enraged that he took a split moment—decision to kill the other person, in cold blood, as he was standing right in front of his car." Priti continued "What has happened to people? Anger, ego arrogance, rivalry have distorted mindsets over time that human life has ceased to be of value?"

Mahesh remarked "That is the core problem! People do not believe in self-change and are busy pointing fingers at others. Take our case! Are we not prone to pointing fingers at Shagun for her behaviour? Why are we doing this? She is our daughter and it is because of our karma in previous lifetimes that we are facing this situation. Our bad acts then, has led us to face this problem in this lifetime.

We need to change ourselves in terms of improving on those traits which are negative and are a intrinsic part of our being. They are anger, ego, arrogance irritability, sulking and begrudging our lives" Priti remarked "There would be very few who would embark on self change, people invariably hold others responsible for their own agonies"

Mahesh continued "You know that only when we bring about a change in ourselves, only then are we in a position to bring about a change in our circumstances."

Mahesh continued "Self change only can lead to a change in the external environment. The process of introspection is indeed difficult as one has to accept one's own drawbacks and then rectify them. It is easier said than done." Priti grinned "In that case, if you were to change, then the best person to confirm that is me. The self change as widely propogated should be first applied at home. That is the acid test as they say"

Mahesh was astounded on hearing Priti "Priti, you are spot on! It is easy to be sweet and nice to strangers, but difficult to make your family members see the difference in you. Hence, they are the best persons to ascertain any positive change in the person. So, are you noticing any positive change in me?" Priti was all smiles and said "Lets wait and watch each other."

This spiritual discussion between a couple can serve the purpose of eye opener to people who are constantly caught in this highly competitive era when it is necessary to pause to fathom, as to, which direction are we heading on a spiritual platform.

Youngsters, too, need to be perceptive to the needs of the times rather than getting swept away by a self-centred approach which is aimed at ambitious achievements by hook or by crook. Priti was talking to Mahesh "In these days of cut-throat competition, the young generation are resorting to anything and everything to promote their professional growth.

I keep hearing this in kitty parties where the topic is only their children and how rapidly times are changing. Offices have become a breeding ground for back biting amongst colleagues, who go to any extent to please their bosses."

Mahesh remarked "This was not the case when I was in a job. There was a lot of friction between colleagues but that did not come in the way of a healthy personal relationship between us. The practical reality is that the working environment has changed and has become far more competitive than before."

Priti reacted "Self change in such an atmosphere is difficult to perceive and tough to actually apply." Mahesh paused "I do not see any other way as the alternatives are mindless and human values will be dumped in the trash-can. I am sure that millions of parents must be facing this problem and would be at a loss to figure out a solution."

Priti added "Newspapers report frequently about young boys and girls of rich and affluent families driving snazzy cars, after taking alcohol and result in terrible accidents. Initially, I used to blame the parents to have given liberties to their children to go for late night parties, and drive after getting drunk.

But, hearing some of these hapless rich parents in social dos' makes it abundantly clear that the children are not in their control." Mahesh reacted "You are right! I used to think the same way but that is not true. I can well imagine their plight when their sons/ daughters would be going out for late night parties as well as the "after parties" how helpless would they be? There are regular instances of ghastly accidents thereafter. Imagine young children gone.!

Any amount of policing is not sufficient! It is all in the mind."

Priti was serious now and said "Mahesh, do you realise that we too have a growing daughter of 16 yrs now! She is anyway disoriented with us! What are we going to do to prevent all this to impact our daughter?" Mahesh smiled "We have to win her over through love and affection, treating her as a friend instead of a grown up daughter. The parental approach will have to change. To do so, we have to change ourselves in her eyes on a daily basis, on a continuous basis."

It was now Priti's turn to smile and say "Mahesh, it is very easy to do high-sounding and well wishing talk but very difficult to apply. Infact, you lose your balance of mind at a slight provocation." Mahesh also smiled "This is a awakening which we have to be conscious off and determined enough to apply. I agree what you are saying is true but you will also agree that it is high time that we wake up too and practice it on a regular basis. We have to support and correct each other whenever necessary"

Priti agreed "We must do this otherwise she too would also be one of the many youngsters we are talking about. We have to use our wisdom, to react from the mind, rather than impulsively, in the heat of the moment. vis-a-vis Shagun."

Mahesh replied "We will be able to use our mind instead of heart only when we genuinely remove our drawbacks which everybody has ie anger, ego arrogance irritability, sulking etc. This has to be applied wrt everybody, not just Shagun, irrespective of cast, creed and status in society. We need to be discreetly compassionate with everybody.

This is what I have understood while reading books on spiritualism."

Priti grinned "You should start delivering lectures on how to lead daily lives! I entirely agree with what you are saying." Mahesh continued "We have to pray with the determination that we are able to change ourselves and use our common sense to show a change in ourselves to everybody. We can then claim to be better human beings." Priti queried "If every human being were to improve oneself, then there would be little difference between us and god almighty. What will then happen to the negative functions in the universe?" Mahesh responded "God is inside us. This is what I read and it appeals to me.

Every human being has godliness inside him and he just has to bring it to the fore. The external environment, also, will then improve and become conducive to us. The negative functions are nothing else but a result of our past karmic actions. We have to fight them, confront them and win thereafter." Priti said "Vow! This is a fantastic logic! And very convincing too. I wish everybody thinks on these lines. We would all be much happier off! Lets go for it! Anything for happiness!" Priti and Mahesh, embarked on the conclusion drawn from the discussion held above to make themselves happy and also normalise their relationship with Shagun by befriending her.

The environment was globally worsening day by day. The rat-race amongst countries to acquire nuclear weapons bears testimony to this thought process. Efforts for global peace have been lost or stalled due to mindless terrorist attacks by people who have their own personal agenda.

Hatred emanating from acts of vengeance can only be mindless! Peace leading to mutual regard and respect amongst all human beings, is the only solution. Mahesh remarked one day "There are certain parts of the world where there is continuous violence throughout the year, year after year. Millions of innocent lives are friterred away in this bloody bath but to no no avail!"

Priti remarked "Peace is a slow and gradual process as it entails change of mindsets. First, people have to understand self change, accept it, and implement it to attempt to bring about harmony amongst all human beings. I am sure there must be millions of likeminded individuals who must be thinking and taking action on the same lines as us. After all, everyone will prefer peace, mutual respect, to disharmony and hatred." Mahesh responded "I completely agree, madam! Women too should command respect which is not the case in many parts of the world."

Mahesh cont'd "Women are at par with men today, a fact which should be accepted by all and sundry. However, in conventional households in rural India, for instance, women are treated as somewhat glorified cooks, a situation which must change as in other parts of the country as well as the world."

Priti was pleased "Keep it up. Mahesh! You are on the right track! I know men have accepted this reality, but not all! Predominantly, men still have orthodox mindsets. Even today, men in Urban Delhi find it difficult to digest women overtaking them in their cars. It is a common sight."

It is commonly seen that people measure the success of an individual from his financial wellbeing rather than his qualities as a human being with a sound value system. People who have palatial houses, a fleet of cars and a successful and flourishing business, command a lot of respect from others. The same individuals may be short tempered, egoistic and arrogant in behaviour with others. Such people who are affluent are otherwise an unhappy lot of people who do not accept other human beings at par.

Priti agreed and said "Most of us get carried away by success in terms of money and status in society and get even more arrogant. The intrinsic behaviour worsens and there are many instances of such people who recklessly indulge in nefarious activities and ruin their so called prestige in society and some amongst them land behind bars" Mahesh added "Once they are financially successful, they become fearless and erroneously assume that they are beyond the reach of law, are caught ultimately and realise their blunders thereafter.

Therefore, the necessity to self change is even more paramount, in view of these people and circumstances. The entire approach to people and society would change and would be replaced by mutual regard and camaraderie. The inner life state would reach a higher level and the the entire perspective of life and its ups and downs would change radically."

Priti while hearing Mahesh was pleasantly surprised and the conviction with which he was talking "Mahesh, when did you acquire this knowhow, and clarity of mind?" Mahesh said "Sweetheart, there comes a time when the mind is searching for spiritual solutions to day to day problems of life. It is then necessary to read and mature in the perspective in which the vagaries of life have to be dealt with."

Mahesh continued "Priti, surely, you must have noticed that I seldom get irritated anymore. In addition to this, I trying to control my temper also." Priti remarked "Maybe, I am your wife, and we are together everyday, that is why I have not noticed any discernible change so far. I will be keenly observing you from now onwards." It was Mahesh's turn to grin "So would I! Priti, your actions would now be under a microscope too."

Mahesh was by nature a short-tempered guy who would get provoked easily. Apart from this, he was prone to get irritated at a slight inconvenience. He was known to lose his temper at his subordinates, if he had left his house in a bad mood. As commonly seen, bosses are known to howl at their staff without any provocation whatsoever! Mahesh used to have a cold frequently and was obviously not in a pleasant mood on reaching office. So, the staff new that they would get a firing any moment.!

Surely, the staff was not responsible for Mahesh's cold. Hence, there was no justification for Mahesh to lose it at them. Similarly, all of us have a natural tendency to hold others responsible for our agonies! It is so wrong! On the contrary, if we exercise self control, the response from our surroundings would be at parity with our well being.

The manner in which we then handle our work would be different and the results too undoubtedly be better, on a relative basis. Likewise, once we exercise self control in the house, the atmosphere would be better and there would be an aura of peace and harmony within the family. If the battle of self-change through self-control is won at the office and home, a predominant part of our problems would be neutralised.

Furthermore, if we are in control of our mindsets, we would be able to think better and use our common sense to solve problems. Anger, ego and arrogance are serious states of mind and lead to negative repercussions only. We have to be mentally tough to be able to first understand and then make efforts to curb them and over time, eliminate them from our systems.

Mahesh while discussing the issues with Priti one day said "I am sure that if we stop reacting impulsively and pause and then react, we would be able to not only remove these negative traits from our personalities but also stop getting irritated, at the drop of a hat!" Priti responded "I agree completely! Also, in the face of life's ups and downs all of us invariably start begrudging and sulking, at our very existence in this lifetime. Then, we end up hating others or envy others who are apparently better off than us, without knowing full details"

Mahesh smiled "Therefore, we need to be more tolerant and exercise self control through self change. All of us can do this as long as we have the faith in our conviction to do so." Priti was quick to reply "Therefore, it is first a matter of our faith in self change and the urge to do so". The readers may note the practical relevance in this discussion which took place between a couple, as above. This is the only solution in the modern day world, of today. If citizens of all countries think alike, all human beings would become better individuals and peace would prevail.

At least, we can all embark on this path of peace and prosperity. It is a process but unless we cleanse our minds and genuinely undertake self-change, we would not be able to take a right step forward. The sense of urgency and the dire need to do so is paramount, considering the state the world is in.

The practical relevance of self change can be better understood from the understanding of the word "karma". Traditionally, karma is taken to be synonymous with action. However, action emanates from a thought process in the mind. It would be more appropriate to define karma as a combination of "thoughts, words and action."

All of us read the newspapers on a daily basis and read about different forms of violence inflicted on children. Surely, readers would agree that it would be reasonable to accept that before becoming majors, these kids would not have undertaken such actions that would justify the kind of serious violence inflicted on them.

Similarly, there are numerous incidents of terrorist attacks which result in loss of innocent lives, apart from various other forms of violence which are spurred by traits like enmity, jealousy, marital disputes ending in deaths, political rivalry-related violence, family-disputes relating to ancestral properties, road rage, accidental deaths, business rivalry, etc and various other forms and causes of violence.

When we sit back and analyse the rationale behind those who were victimised, it will not be difficult to comprehend that these situations could be a aftermath of our karma of previous lifetimes.

Hence, we need to change the karmic consequences of past deeds through a methodology which would appeal to all, across the globe. There can be no magical solution to these situations. It can happen through changing our inner selves to be able to accept and own responsibility for our circumstances in this lifetime.

As and when we start practising inner-change we would be able to develop regard and respect for all human beings, irrespective of caste and creed. The world would then become a better place to live in. Moreover, once we start purifying ourselves, we will surely notice that our external environment is also responding to us. We would then embark on a path of indulging in pure thoughts, words and actions and improving our present as well as our future.

As an example, Mahesh had stopped reacting to those drivers who were in a hurry to overtake on the road and, instead had started smiling at them. He was narrating this to Priti one day who remarked "Do not start smiling at all female drivers who may complain to the police and you can be hauled up." Mahesh had a hearty laugh. He further told Priti "In most of the cases my smile was reciprocated with a smile. Initially, I was surprised as it was quite unlike earlier occasions when I used to hurl abuses at those who flouted traffic rules and not follow driving discipline. But, that always used to leave a bad taste in the mouth."

Priti grinned "We have been a witness to this trait of your's but used to keep mum because that would have enraged you further. I used to be very frightened when, at times, you used to get into an argument with the other person. Those were impulsive moments when anything could have happened, at the spur of the moment, I used to be petrified at the thought of it, as we are used to reading incidents of this kind repeatedly in the past. The situation seems to be worsening day by day."

Mahesh hung his head in shame "Priti, I cannot undo what I have already done, but can assure you that I will not do the same again. Just realising my drawback is not enough, you will see me smiling frequently and not get into any brawls anymore. In fact, you can try the same in being more understanding with the maids who broom the house as well as for other jobs in the house. I am sure you will notice a change in their response as well."

"I will certainly try your self-change mode and report back to you, boss" said Priti. Mahesh further elaborated "I will try hard not to be in an irritable mood before going to office as well as after coming back, as you've seen on a routine basis. Irritation is a form of sulkng and I have no right to sulk at you for no rhyme or reason." Priti was genuinely pleased to hear this.

She also realised that she would have to raise the bar of her own level of tolerance so that she can handle Shagun and Kiran better. She told Mahesh "I will equally reciprocate! You will see the difference in me in several parameters. Lets also tell others as well so that they can slowly and gradually improve on all fronts." "Right, maam" was Mahesh's response. Mahesh started experiencing the joy in communicating with more compassion for others even if it is a maid in the house or a peon who does sundry jobs in office.

In office, one day he enquired about the wellbeing of the employee, and was shocked to find that the peon burst out crying as he was in the midst of severe family problems. He did not expect anything from Mahesh but profusely thanked him for being receptive to his problems. Mahesh felt an unusual calm which descended on him and the resulting happiness had made his day. He promptly narrated this to Priti who was overjoyed. Mahesh also observed that if the day in office starts off on a happy note then the mental faculties are better to face the challenges on a daily basis, if any.

Likewise, Priti told Mahesh one day "Today my maid was unwell. So, unlike ever before, I asked her to have a cup of tea. She was astonished and kept staring at me for some time, when I told her again to have tea. She had it and then told me that she was thrilled to be treated as a normal human being." Mahesh was exhilarated. Suddenly, the thought process was buoyant and optimistic for the future and the attitude was positive.

A little compassion with mutual regard for each other when practised on a daily basis can do wonders.! There are instances of families with internal bickerings can easily get solved with mutual consensus, provided our mind is at peace with ourselves. Dialogue plays an important role and the respect for others can convert hatred into compassion. This is possible if small changes, as cited above, are inculcated in the daily routine. This process of self transformation can invite common prudence to come to the minds of people, to successfully tackle our set of problems.

We must realise that we must try and improve ourselves to an extent that people are drawn towards us and our ways of conducting ourselves in society on a daily basis. Family bickerings emanate fron our self-centredness and pursuit of selfish motives only.

In such situations, as Priti was once mentioning to Mahesh, "Every action has an equal and opposite reaction. The manner in which we communicate would be also reciprocated equally and oppositely. When we view this in the case of these differences amongst family members, this aspect has direct relevance. We must learn to respect and accept each other's inherent godliness or goodness. Dialogue laced with logic can be acceptable. The alternative is scary and invariably turns out to be disastrous." Mahesh reacted "In such situations, we should try our level best. Beyond this, if things turn awry, we will still have the satisfaction that our path was right.

The principle of self change and mutual respect applies to politics at a global level. As Mahesh was mentioning to Priti "Politicians are in a desperate pursuit of their personal agenda, devoid of the larger objective of improving the wellbeing of the society as a whole. Political governance and accountability should have a social objective as well.

The innumerous schemes of govts for improving the financial condition of the people can be more meaningful if people are educated in undertaking self improvement on a daily basis to be able to improve their own life state and be more tolerant and be able to successfully handle their own problems on a day-to-day basis." Priti responded "Mahesh, it is not so simple for people to own responsibility for their own circumstances and try to sort it out through self-change.

People adopt the easier alternative of holding others responsible for their agonies and take what they already have for granted. It is very important to express gratitude to the almighty and feel content about the same. There is no harm in having desires but we should not sulk about the non-achievement of the same."

Mahesh was pleasantly surprised "Amazing! Your understanding is crystal clear! We can only hope that people should awaken to this reality and actually apply it in their lives. Their entire perception would undergo a sea-change reg handling negative situations."

The previous decades had actually undergone drastic changes in every sphere of life and so had people's perceptions. Money-power has become a focal point in the lives of office-goers, entrepreneurs, political parties. The appetite for financial betterment has made the going highly competitive for people working in offices in all types of organisations.

While employees go to any extent to please their superiors, the employers are entirely focussed on profit as their only objective. Such an environment makes the industrial atmosphere very competitive, leading to undesire able situations which to resorting to unfairpractices. The objective is to win at all costs, by hook or crook. Hence, it is logical to find people getting frustrated on being dissatisfiedwith their achievements. Crime, in such a environment, also rises phenomenally."

Readers may note that the passage of time has drastically changed the very definition of life, in all its facets. We must also realise that we have to also upgrade our spirituality in handling this highly fiercely competitive environment, to be at par with the fast changing times. We must introspect, undertake self improvement and actually improve our daily lives. As explained earlier, this can be practically applied and results would validate this thought process.

Having explained the contents of the changing times and its impact on daily lives of people, lets now move into the mainstream of Mahesh's family and how, alongwith Priti, he copes up with the fast growing Shagun and Kiran and what the family has to under go in terms of interpersonal relationships and the parental battle to face the emotional ups and downs and how they are able to win over those situations, through perseverence and raising their bar of tolerance, using their common prudence, at the same time.

Chapter 8

"Do not meddle in my life",
"I am not a kid anymore"

Mahesh was only trying to engage Shagun in a conversation. The response was most unjustified! Shagun was now 21 yrs of age and had finished her courses in fashion & textile designing and had gained experience in her field with reputed names in the fashion industry in India. She got tremendous appreciation from those whom she worked with.

Having gained in experience, she decided to set up her own brand and started making her own garments as well as fashion accessories, taking help of her circle of friends whom she had cultivated over the previous couple of years. She had already started projects from well known companies in the fashion industry. As a step in this direction, she opened up a place in a prime area, which served as an office and meeting point as well as a store to display of various wares of different designers. The marketing of the place was done through facebook, direct marketing techniques etc.

Shagun's initiatives in promoting her career prospects were indeed admirable. Mahesh and Priti did not have any role play in setting her up as the nature of her work was vastly different from Mahesh's nature of business. Realising this, Shagun had become egoistic& arrogant, and this reflected in her interactions with her parents.

Priti mentioned this to Mahesh "Shagun's attitude towards us has worsened in the last five years. The bonding between us has touched an unusual low." Mahesh replied "Actually, despite our best efforts, she felt isolated after Kiran's birth. It was an unavoidable situation and it was impossible to strike a perfect balance between Shagun and Kiran in terms of the time devoted to them. Both of us were preoccupied, you in the house with Kiran and me in the office due to fluctuations in the market.

What could we do?" Priti responded "However, we must nicely and politely but firmly, if necessary, keep up a dialogue with her so as to try and improve the situation, without her feeling that we are not giving her space and are meddling in her affairs." Mahesh responded "Look at how the times have changed! In our younger days, although I used to have a difference of opinion with our parents, not once did we ridicule them or told them not to interfere in our matters."

"I agree," Priti said and continued "We were much more disciplined also and did not have the cheek to get into a heated argument with parents." "Very correct, parenting is not an easy job" said Mahesh. Little did poor Mahesh and

Priti realise what was in store for them. Shagun's attitude kept worsening.

She used to keep making fun of the fact that her mother was not a working person and hence she had no locus-standii to comment on her official matters. Mahesh, with some degree of difficulty had to explain to her that it is entails an equal amount of responsibility to look after the house in comparison to an office.

Shagun retorted "Papa, you think you know everything! You have no clue about what I am doing and it would be better if you mind your affairs which too you are not able to do." Mahesh and Priti who was standing closeby were dumbstruck! Such ego and what way of talking to the parents! Priti retaliated "Shagun, this is no way to talk to your father. He is simply talking to you out of concern" Pat came the reply "Mom, you stay out of this, stop meddling in my affairs, I am not a kid anymore, you go and do your kitchen work." Hearing this, Mahesh lost it! "Shagun you have become an insolent over ripe kid! Behave yourself! Otherwise, the going will be tough for you"

It was now Shagun's turn to retort "What will you do?" Mahesh replied "Do you realise that I am bearing yr credit card expenses, yr mobile bill, yr car Emi, and a host of other expenses on a regular basis. The least I expect you is to behave yourself with your parents" "Just go away from my room "Shagun replied and added "If you could not take care of children why did you have children in the first place? Go away now"

Mahesh and Priti walked out thoroughly enraged at Shagun's utterances. Priti was speechless and later broke down crying! Mahesh kept mum and seeing Priti cry, was trying to comfort her. Kiran who was 15 yrs now could perceive that her sister was the culprit. In broken language, she conveyed to her parents that she would set her sister right. She promptly walked to her sister's room and reprimanded her for her misbehaviour with her parents. She however did not receive any firing from her elder sister.

This interaction between the parents was one of the many instances of the complete breakdown of rapport between the parents and Shagun. The situation worsened as she grew in her career making her egoistic, arrogant and self-centred. Her mannerisms too worsened. She developed an extreme sense of finickiness in her likes and dislikes for different dishes cooked in the house.

She had developed liking for junk-food, wafers, fried potato fingers and roasted snacks all the time. Priti was widely appreciated for her cooking abilities, in dinner parties hosted in their house. Shagun, on the other hand, ridiculed her preparations, more because of her disliking for the fact that Mahesh, as the father was invariably siding with Priti, for correct reasons.

In the meantime, due to perhaps a sense of insecurity in the house, Shagun had developed a liking for a boy she was frequently meeting every other day. As parents, Mahesh and Priti were quite forward looking and did not find anything amiss in a friendly relationship which Shagun was having with a boy who was her age.

What was disturbing was the frequency of the meetings and at odd hours. As parents, Mahesh and Priti could not ignore the situation and had to communicate with her.

Priti, one day, brought up the topic at dinnertime. She asked "Shagun, are you seeing a man?" Prompt came the reply "It is none of your business!" Mahesh intervened "Your mother is simply asking a question, she is neither arguing with you nor is she upset with you! Why can't you give a proper reply?"

She replied "Okay, I like him and we are in a relationship" Mahesh responded "Be careful, that is all we expect you to do. Also, familiarity breeds contempt! Meet him but not as frequently as you are!"

Mahesh continued "Shagun, the frequency with which you are meeting him would result in differences and would spoil the relationship. This would hurt you as well. I am not saying this because I do not want you to meet him. I am not discouraging you in anyway." What Shagun then had to say astounded both Mahesh and Priti! She said "Whether my relationship with him continues or not is none of your business and whether I live or die should not bother you also."

Priti then chipped in! "You are our elder daughter, how can you say all this, what has your father said which has provoked this thought in your mind. I am shocked!" Shagun then left her room and went out of the house. It was 10pm. Mahesh went after her and told her firmly to come back immediately. She came inside and locked herself in her room. Kiran, who was watching the proceedings immediately rushed to the room which was shared by both of them, imploring upon Shagun to open the room. After about half an hour, the room was opened.

In the meantime, the parents walked back to their room, deciding not to continue the conversation with Shagun.

Both kept quiet for some time. It was a rude shock! This is the force of karma and they had to deal with it. Mahesh finally spoke "This is an indication of things to come. The situation has uncontrollably worsened over the preceding years. But, we have to deal with it and overcome it." Priti remarked "How? The manner in which she is reacting almost gives me the impression that we need to take her to a psychiatrist who can understand the root cause of the problem and counsel her accordingly." Mahesh smiled "Do you think that she would agree? Or are you suggesting that we should use force and somehow take her.?" "No, no no, Priti remarked, how can I suggest this? What is the solution otherwise?"

Mahesh said "Self change, as we had discussed earlier! She is not behaving like this with everybody. Had she developed a mental malfunction, she would have been talking crazy stuff with all and sundry. We will have to over time inculcate love and affection in our relationship with her, despite provocation by her. As normal human beings it will take us a lot of time as we are not ready for actually applying it. At least we can make an effort! "Priti replied "I agree but till the time we actually improve our bonding with her, it will be very difficult to digest her rubbish!"

Shagun had also developed weird habits like lying down on the sofa in the living room, despite the fact that Priti had on innumerous times, reprimanded her not to do so. It almost appeared that Shagun was doing this deliberately to incur Priti's wrath. Priti strongly felt that the living room area should be properly kept rather than in a dishevelled state, as all visitors come and sit there.

However, Shagun continued to lie down there. Priti had to resist the urge to lose her temper at her. Seeing her sister doing this, Kiran started to do the same and lie down on the other sofaset in the living room. Priti was enraged and rang up Mahesh in the office to convey this to him.

Mahesh simply told her "Look Priti, you will have to correct her politely otherwise you would end up encouraging her to continue doing this" Priti now had Mahesh's moral support and decided to talk to Shagun as politely as possible. "I have told you so many times that you should not lie down on the sofa in living room and you are continuing to do the same! Seeing you Kiran is doing the same! What is wrong with you? Have you decided not to listen to yr mother?"

Pat came the reply "Yes, try and throw me out" Priti was clueless and how to react. Keeping in mind what Mahesh and her had discussed the previous day, she kept mum, controlled her anger and walked away.

Shagun was getting unmanageable! Priti narrated the incident to Mahesh when he came back from office. Promptly, he went to Shagun's room and told her "If you cannot behave yourself, why don't you stay somewhere else? I will pay for your boarding and lodging. Start looking for an alternative accomodation!" Shagun retorted "I am not going anywhere, this is my house also."

Mahesh told her "I am warning you! I will have to shift you to a mental asylum." Shagun gave it back "Try and do this and I will call the cops and malign you all over facebook and all other social mediums." Mahesh now had completely lost it and said "Now onwards, do not ask me for any financial help of any kind, you have crossed all limits! Does your boyfriend know how you behave with yr parents.? He will leave you!"

On hearing this, Shagun went mad and said "In that case, I will kill myself and hold you responsible!"

Mahesh, as earlier, was stunned! He did not know what to say! He quickly retraced his steps and went back to his room. He recollected his earlier days when he was Shagun's age. There was not even a singular instance of misbehaviour of this magnitude. Had his parents been around, they would have been shell-shocked and would have held both Mahesh and Priti for this situation.

Was their something wrong in their upbringing? Or were they victims of the fast changing times or was it the force of their karma of previous lifetimes? There were no ready answers! Priti chipped in "What's happening? Had I known these repercussions, I would never have agreed to have children. This is crazy! I am sure that in the entire universe this would not be happening in all families! The atmosphere of our house has been ruined completely. All this is impacting Kiran as well. What will her special mind make out of interpersonal relationships?"

Mahesh reminded her of similar situations existing in innumerous families. He narrated to her about a family in Singapore where there were acute relationship problems which existed between the in-laws on one side and the son and the daughter-in-law, on the other. This was when the parents were most accomodating, devoid of any foul language exchanged between all of them. A situation had developed whereby there was practically no communication between all of them. One can imagine the extent of disharmony in their house.

With the passage of time, the situation had worsened to such an extent that the son and daughter-in-law would remain closeted in the room, all the time. In case they were going out of station or coming back, no greetings were exchanged and they had started operating as paying-guests in the house. While the daughter-in-law had no contribution in the house in any matter, the son who had been brought up in the same house had turned truant and had started misbehaving and ignoring the parents. There had been no heated exchanges in the past but there were differences of opinion on certain matters relating to the house.

Rather than sorting them out, the children decided to adopt the path of least resistance by reducing communication to the minimal extent. Do parents not have a right to discuss certain issues with their children and try and take remedial action? In earlier times, this was certainly not the case. It cannot be a tit-for-tat policy with elders and children alike. Today it appears that children retort back spontaneously to any reprimands of the parents, without the slightest amount of hesitation, very unlike earlier generations.

Mahesh told Priti "The family I am referring to now are faced with a situation that to restore peace and harmony in the house the parents are forced to ask their children to live separately. The children, on the other hand, realising their selfish interests have refused to move out.

The young couple are career oriented individuals and expect their parents to take care of the ensuing arrival of their grandchild. While the prospective grandparents instead of being excited about the new arrival are more apprehensive about the continued misdemeanour of their grown up career minded children."

The lack of communication has led to absence of cordiality in the atmosphere, and there remains an uneasy silence in their house. I have started wondering whether our house is moving in that direction." Priti has been brooding on the same lines and replied "the way things are going in our house is a wake-up call for us, but what can be do about it."

Mahesh replied "This is the situation with millions of families all over the world. There is no readymade solution before us."

The contents so far in this chapter were more focussed on the quality of interaction between Shagun and her parents with Kiran, a special girl being a witness to it. Shagun, in the last 5 years had grown to be closer to her friends and not her parents. This was attributable to that fact that post-Kiran's birth, she felt sidelined and was at peace in her circle of friends and slowly and gradually this bent of mind took roots in her mind.

In the last 5 years, the daily interactions had reduced substantially and further created the divide amongst them. The usage of a swanky mobile had contributed to this situation. The extent of usage and time spent on using it was amazing! There was a time when she would sit on the dining table for dinner, everybody was asked to keep quiet and she would finish her dinner, talking to her friend. There were times when Mahesh would tell her not to talk while having dinner. In response, she would gesture to him to keep quiet. On one occasion, on being reprimanded again for this act of misbehaviour, Mahesh was asked not to interfere.

The situation had reached a stage that to maintain peace, the parents had to keep their mouths shut just to enable Shagun to freely communicate with her friend, at dinnertime. "What is happening?" Thought Priti? Apart from this, Shagun would be busy with the laptop, irrespective of the time of the day or night. Priti while checking up on them on a routine basis, once daily in the wee hours of the morning would invariably find her busy.

Shagun had started sleeping late and getting up around 1pm everyday, and then get ready for the day and leave for her office. Her frequent monetary requirements were routed through crisp smses every other day to her father Mahesh used to ask her about the purpose of the money required only to be told that he should not enquire about the reason and simply say "yes" or "no" as to whether he would pay or not. There were no feelings in the interaction!

Similarly, Priti would simply ask her if she wanted any snack in office or not? Shagun would reply in a yes or no and would never bother to enquire about what she would be giving! Priti also decided, seeing the nature of the communication not to ask her if she needed a snack or not and would wait for her to actually request her for the same. Likewise, Mahesh told Priti "I agree with you and would do the same reg the money she keeps taking from me. She is taking both of us for granted! While parents think the best for their children, it is vitally important that they are not taken for granted on the premise that this is a duty which they have to discharge just because they are the ones who gave birth to them."

Beyond a certain age, they should ideally live separately and ekk out their own living or else it cuts both ways wherein the children and the parents have to adjust with each other in peace and harmony. Parents belonging to different generations also need to evolve and recognise that we are living in an age of vastly improved technology whereby youngsters have access to fast and a variety of social mediums on the net as well as television and are used to a very fast moving professional and personal life.

In the instant case, it appears that Shagun was having best of all the worlds in terms of having a relationship with a man, lead a self centred existence where she is free to lead a life of her own within the confines of the house which was managed by her parents. There was no reciprocity from Shagun in terms of a basic miminum display of regard and respect towards her parents who were just yearning for this.

As the times were progressing, a stage was developing when there would be no bonding left between the parents and children and there would be minimal communication between all of them. Hence, the parents were correct in strategising that Shagun should not be given a free hand in the expenses being incurred on her just to make her realise that it is a two way process and she was required to reciprocate as well.

Mahesh told Priti "As a father, I am faltering in fulfilling all her requirements financially especially when she is on her own and should actually derive her livelyhood from her own sources of income. Alternatively, she should explain why she is expecting her father to foot her bills while she continues to be so insolent towards to both of them."

Priti responded "It will not be easy! She will utter such gibberish that to avoid spoiling the atmosphere, you would give in to her demands." Mahesh smiled "I will start using my mind now onwards and stop reacting from the heart. In order to do so, I do not have to lose my temper. Let us try it out."

It was only a day later that Mahesh was required to pay for her mobile which ran into a couple of thousand rupees. He called her and told her to pay for her bill. The look on Shagun's face was full of scorn and contempt rather than apprehension. She simply heard him and walked back to her room.

Priti continued "While I agree that she should be made to learn so that she mends her ways and face reality, will it help to bring things to this point?" Mahesh replied "how else do we make her realise? Let us use our minds rather than reacting emotionally. She has taken us for granted assuming that it is our parental duty to take care of all her needs, despite the fact that shi is already earning independently through her free-lance projects.

Whenever I try to engage her in a conversation, she snubs me and tells me not to interfere. Incase she is in some sort of a temporary problem, are we not the ones who form her fall-back mechanism, and try and help her out?" Priti responded "Certainly! I only want that she should not feel isolated." Shagun was regularly requiring money for her requirements without explaining the reason or any info about how much she was earning.

Moreover, her behaviour was atrocious only with them and she would be very sweet in her interactions with everyone else. She had a habit to buy branded clothes and would discard them after a couple of times. What utter wastage of money! Not all garments need to be linked to some well known brand only! The cost is more because of the brand image only, while similar clothes are available elsewhere.

Moreover, she would, as per her mother would also sleep in the night wearing the same clothes, other wise meant for party wear. This was ridiculous! It so emerges that not only her behaviour but her habits were also undergoing a change for the worse. Despite nearing the age of 22 yrs, she was obstinate enough not to lay her bed also, expecting her mother to do so.

Her perception of her mother had changed and she viewed her as a glorified maidservant whose job was to cook, look after the house and do anything and everything to fulfill the children's requirements. This attitude got developed ever since Shagun started working and managing her own venture. Moreover, she always noticed that her father was in agreement with her mother and this aspect probably felt her even more insecure. However, her immature mind further estranged her from her mother through a sea change in her attitude towards her.

Shagun made frequent trips outside the city to participate in exhibitions, the expenses of which were borne by her father in terms of airfare, boarding and lodging expenses, though the trips were entirely to promote her own business expenses.

Mahesh used to think that this would help in her career, at this stage, but never anticipated that instead of having the feeling of gratitude for her father, she would worsen in her behaviour towards her parents. Hence, it was high time that Shagun be made to realise her mistakes so as to ensure that she matures in the times to come and not take parental help for granted.

Shagun's requests for money were turned down and was told to manage through her own sources. She was apparently taken by surprise but became even more antagonistic towards them. A couple of days later when the due date for payment of the credit Card had passed, she chose to approach her father again only to be told to manage on her own. Shagun responded "You can't even help at this early stage of my career, what sort of father are you?"

Mahesh replied when Priti was also around "What sort of daughter are you? The least we expect from you is that you should feel happy about what is being done for you and only behave yourself with us and not give cryptic replies to us whenever we talk to you on any matter." Shagun replied "How do you behave with me, you are always correcting me or curbing me for something or the other, I am fed up!" Mahesh replied "We have always nicely tried to explain to you out of concern for you and have never insulted you or reprimanded you for no rhyme or reason! We are your fall-back mechanism and you do not have this realisation"

Priti also intervened "Have be objected to your friendship with a man? You have treated me with contempt on several occasions! Have I rebuked you for your extreme misbehaviour, even once? We are your parents and think only of your welfare and are deeply concerned and touched by your rude behaviour." Kiran was watching the scene attentively, and realised that Shagun had to mend her ways. So, she also chipped in "Sis, PL understand and be sweet to your parents." Pat came the reply "Just shut up, Kiran and get out from here." Kiran was determined "I will not! They are my parents, also." Hearing this, Mahesh and Priti could not help grinning.! Shagun was enraged! She said "You both are smiling! This is sheer rubbish!"

Mahesh responded "We are a little amused at Kiran's reaction just because it is unexpected from a special girl you which seem to have forgotten" Shagun was in no mood to admit her mistake and promptly walked to her room. Just as they sat down to take time to reflect on the interaction, Shagun was back, this time with the most unusual request in recent times. She said "I want to do a one year's course in Paris from a reputed institute of fashion designing to further my career prospects."

Mahesh asked "Who is going to look after your office cum retail outlet.? Do you expect me to foot the expenses on account of yr course for one year and boarding and lodging expenses, which may collectively be a substantial amount. I cannot afford to do so." Shagun replied "How are other parents managing? You cannot do anything!" Mahesh said "I am already managing your expenses when actually you should be bearing them because you are doing well but choose to blow up the money on shopping on yourself.

Alternatively, you should close down this outlet and look up a job where you can get a fat salary, based on yr qualifications and experience." The readers may note Shagun's audacity without any realisation whatsoever for the expenses already been borne by her parents, how self-centred can she be?

The extent of selfishness is unfathomable! In our earlier days, we were always conscious of the fact that our parents are doing their best for us and we used to bear a sense of gratitude towards them rather than nursing ill feelings towards them for airy-fairy desires which remained unfulfilled. Never did we have the guts or the motivation to confront our parents and be insolent towards them in any manner.

The world seems to have undergone a radical change in terms of the successive generations, their outlook towards life and the skyhigh expectations and ambitions they cherish. Priti used to frequently talk to Mahesh on this matter and how they would be able to secure a stable future for Kiran. She said "I am very circumspect about Shagun's ability to be able to take care of Kiran when we are not around. It requires a lot of patience and perseverence which only a mother can discharge, but I doubt if Shagun, despite the bond which exists between the two sisters today, will be in a position to sustain once she gets married. The priorities change and because of all round pressure, to also manage the demanding requirements of a handicapped sister is next to impossible."

Mahesh had this thought in his mind for quite some time and was keen on talking to Priti on the matter. He said "Priti, I agree with you completely! As time is passing, I am more and more getting convinced that Shagun neither has the maturity nor the capacity to take care of Kiran at a later stage when it is required. She may mature as she grows older but once she is married and has children, her preoccupations will increase and even if she wanted to, she would not be able to find the time to do so."

Priti was nonplussed "In that case, whom do we rely upon for this onerous responsibility? As of now, we are very preoccupied in handling Shagun's affairs. We cannot stop thinking about Kiran's future!" Mahesh did not have any ready answers and said "Lets live in the present, have hope for the future and pray that whatever happens is right for Kiran. What else can we do!" Priti said "That is wishful thinking! Sounding like all is well that ends well!"

This time Mahesh got a trifle irritated and said "Priti, why get bogged down when we do not have ready answers! Human values have got heavily eroded and it is difficult to rely on people. We have a fairly big circle of relatives but all said and done we cannot impose a responsibility on anyone." Shagun, on the other hand was conscious of this responsibility and used to harp on it with her parents, at times, with a sense of obligation which she is required to discharge, at a later point in life.

As of now she was completely focussed on herself, her career and her boyfriend. Priti, as a concerned mother mentioned to Mahesh "While we are being forward looking and giving Shagun her space, as is being done the world over, don't you think that we need to know basic things about this boyfriend of hers'?" Mahesh started laughing "Should I deploy the service of private detective to keep stalking Shagun? She cuts of the communication as and when you or I have tried to talk to her about him. These days this is a common practice and their relationship is not serious enough, as she says, in terms of tying the knot."

Priti remarked "Do we then simply accept the situation the way it is?" Mahesh seriously remarked "There is one way where we do not have to incur any costs and we can still unearth the truth about her boyfriend. I can take a couple of days off from my dreary routine, disguise ourselves, get rejuvenated and introduce some excitement in our lives, trail him and get details about him! Are you game for this?"

Priti this time got irritated "Mahesh, you are belittling a potentially explosive situation! We may have to repent for this! We cannot afford to go to the other extreme and take it so casually as you doing." Mahesh decided to comfort her and said "I will take initiative and tell a guy from my office to get some details about him. Ok?" Mahesh was aware that Priti was under pressure from both Kiran and Shagun. There was no point in pushing a matter too far! Kiran's future was exclusively their responsibility and they could not shy away from reality.

As time passed, it was rare to find Shagun accompanying the family to even have a meal together. She would either come back from office and stay indoors, busy with her laptop or with her mobile. On a day-to-day basis, she would take her dinner, the only meal they could have together, and have it in her room. She was also developing dislike for whatever her mother cooked and would have order something from outside, have some from it amd throw away the remaining food in the dustbin.

Mahesh was constrained to reprimand her and said "Shagun, there are people who do not get anything to eat and here are you throwing it away.! This is unacceptable! You are anyway wasting money by not having what is cooked for us and compounding it by throwing away the leftovers from what you ordered from outside." Shagun just shrugged her shoulders and said "What mom cooks is not of my liking! I cannot stuff food in my tummy just because it is ordered from a joint closeby. I will pay for it, so do not worry!" She had also stopped visiting relatives' houses with her parents and would be busy socialising with her boyfriend or else she would frequently see movies with her friends. So, there was perpetually a unhappy atmosphere in the house and her parents at times wondered whether this would be the case, the world over.

There ceased to be bonding at all within the family! Where was the world leading to? Every morning when the family used to wake up, Shagun used to be in deep slumber as she would invariably sleep late and would hate it when Kiran would be woken up in the morning for school., as both of them were sharing the same room. Both the parents had to be particularly careful in not disturbing Shagun or else face a situation when she would shout on being disturbed early in the morning. It is extremely unhealthy for a dismal start to a new day.

The readers may also note that Shagun was a completely different person when it came to communicating with others on a personal or a professional level. Her acquaintances would not have the faintest idea about how she would be behaving with her family. Mahesh had frequently noticed while coming back together home in the evening with her when she would get client calls and from the professionalism she displayed in the phone.

It was evidently clear that her pent up disillusionment was directed towards the family which represented a sitting target for her. Priti and Mahesh were an extremely worried couple whenever they thought of her marriage at some point of time and the extent of adjustment she would be required to do in a completely new set up which would entail just the other spouse or/and the spouse's family as well. A person who due to bad behaviour, mannerisms, habits, finickiness about food would not be an easy person to deal with. Moreover, she was shorttempered and moody and would not be an easy life companion to live a life, what to talk of the traits of the other person, post marriage.

Mahesh said "Marriage is a process of mutual adjustment wherein both the partners have to take equal initiative to make the marriage work. Priti, there are increasing number of instances in the recent past in which we have read that the marriage breaks off due to clash of egos soon after the knot was tied. The breakoff is bound to have a psychological impact od the breaking partners when they contemplate getting into a relationship again." Priti commented "I agree. In order to facilitate that process as far as Shagun is concerned I do not see her adjusting to anybody when she is not in a position to mend her ways with her own parents."

Mahesh responded "A step in that direction for us to soften her and her behavioural problems is for her to see the change in us despite her traits which are unusual as well as her outrageous mannerisms.

As we discussed, in the previous chapter, self change is the only answer on a global level, as this issue would be rampant the world over. We would have to use our minds to react with our minds, in day to day situations, and not impulsively." Priti reacted "That means that we will have to be highly tolerant to her affronts, and persevere all along. That is a huge asking!"

Mahesh continued "There will be provocations all along but we have to pause and react, with our minds." That evening the family had to go to a relatives' place for dinner and Shagun, for once, also trudged along, though unwillingly. Casual conversations were on and soon one of her uncles started asking Mahesh about Shagun's welfare.

She was also standing closeby and talking to one of her cousins. Soon, she intervened and said "Uncle, I will be able to explain better about my affairs as papa does not know much." In that split moment, Mahesh was quick enough to recollect what had been discussed earlier with Priti about self-change and said "Shagun is doing very well, but her field of is in sharp contrast to my field. So, she is right in saying that she would be able to explain better."

Hearing this, there was a look of satisfaction on her face and she nodded to her father in approval. Mahesh was exhilarated! It was as if he had achieved a victory of sorts! He moved away and beckoned to Priti "I could not wait to tell you that the aspect of self change works perfectly when put into practice. You try the same!." "Fantastic" said Priti maybe this is the solution. Lets try it out with immediate effect." The family went back home in a happy state of mind.

While driving back, both Priti and Mahesh had the pleasure of hearing Shagun thanking her father for what he had to say for Shagun in the party. Later in the room, Priti told Mahesh "It was surprising to hear Shagun thank you for praising her in the party. But, when have we not done this in front of relatives or friends? How she behaves with us is our own family matter. Since that is the case why did she thank you today?" Mahesh replied "Maybe the manner in which, I put it across to her uncle is what was appreciated by her. However, you are right that we have praised her, in front of her, earlier also. Time and its passing by will confirm that."

Time, the biggest healing factor, passed and one fine day, it was late in the evening that Shagun approached Mahesh and asked "Papa, I am going out with my friend for dinner" Mahesh asked "Are you telling me or asking me? If you are asking me then let me tell you that its late, and raining hard and it is not advisable for you to go on your own as the chauffeur is gone for the day." Shagun replied "I am a grown up and I have faith on my boyfriend as well, if that is your worry." Mahesh irritatingly said "Why today when it is raining so hard, I am not stopping you from meeting him, but why not tomorrow? I fail to understand why you can't see reason in this!" "I am going today only" said Shagun, who then walked away.

Priti was shocked when she heard this and remarked "This is, perhaps, the reason why she thanked you yesterday, as she wanted you to agree with her unreasonable request today. Mahesh responded "Maybe you are right! But I feel that both the things are not related. She could have avoided thanking me and yet just told us that she was going! She has done this so many times! What could we do?"

The readers may kindly note that Shagun was not off her rockers and was known as a very sweet girl amongst friends and relatives. Her traits in the house were not acceptable by any standards. Her sense of logic and rationale behind her actions was difficult to reason out, it could be attributed to the growing generation gap which was required to be bridged.

Readers may also note that Mahesh and Priti were conscious of giving space to Shagun, did not interfere in anything and and were very forward looking in matters relating to her business or even her set of friends. Times had changed and what was applicable to them in their earlier days was now redundant in terms of mindsets. At the global level, times were evolving and children beyond a certain age were given their own space and they have a world of their own. In the case of this family, Shagun, chose to behave differently with them, extremely cordially with all others. Mahesh and Priti cannot be held guilty of a faulty upbringing of their children.

With the further passage of time, it dawned upon Shagun that she should learn driving to be independent. Both her parents were in agreement that she should learn from a driving school. She, on the other hand, assumed that her father who had tremendous experience would be easily able to help me in doing so. Hence, she approached her father who readily agreed to her desire to learn driving. He was, however in for a surprise when she asked "Papa, then when do we start?"

Taken by surprise, Mahesh said "I will have to check with the driving school who have the people who are trained to impart driving skills to learners." This time it was Shagun's turn to be surprised and said "Papa, lets not waste money as you can easily make me learn driving." Papa replied "There is a tremendous difference between a trainer training you in comparison to my teaching you. Why do you worry in any case? I will pay for this also in addition to the instalment of the car which I am already paying, the fuel cost and now one-time driving classes. I will fix it up for you."

Shagun was upset and said "Papa, one day I will pay you for all this! Do not always keep reminding me of this! You are the father, it is your duty!" Mahesh smiled "Sweetheart, you start behaving properly, respect your mother who has taken care of you since birth, develop good habits, and I will not utter a word to you about our expenses on you, especially when you are earning well. Moreover, pl understand that globally, when children become adults, they need to live an independent life and earning a living which should be sufficient to meet their own expenses. You may not like it but you are having best of both the worlds, one yr own about which you do not want to talk about and one where your parents are bearing a majority of your expenses. It is not the parents duty for an entire lifetime to take care of their children just because they have given birth to them. PL be very clear about this. You can discuss this matter with your friends."

Shagun was not prepared for Mahesh's reaction and had assumed that he would immediately respond and she would start her learning and would be able to able to quickly start driving. Mahesh spoke to a driving school and fixed a time everyday before noon when she would be trained for an hour everyday and would be taking classes for a period of 15 days. He informed Shagun accordingly.

The next day onwards she was getting up on time, showing the earnestness to learn driving as fast as possible, the next two days she attended the classes while the third day she was not ready on time to attend the driving lesson. In the evening when Mahesh returned from office, he enquired from her about her progress in learning the basics of driving. She replied "Papa, these people do not know how to teach! It is a waste of time and money!"

Mahesh was amazed! He told her "You are, at best, a learner when it comes to driving. How can you afford to comment on the trainer. They have been teaching hundreds of learners! Let me talk to them. In the meantime, do not skip a single class! Mahesh took the initiative to to speak to the specific person who was training her. The trainer said that Shagun was not concentrating on learning the basics and instead was being critical of him in his training skills.

Mahesh apologised to him and decided to give a piece of his mind to Shagun. On returning from office, he told Shagun that if she wants to drive one day she will have to be disciplined enough to learn from the same person otherwise she will never be allowed to be given the car for driving ever.

Shagun had no option this time to give a off-the-cuff reply to Mahesh and simply agreed to whatever he had said. It was with great difficulty that Shagun had completed her driving lessions. So, one day the family decided to go to a friend's place in the evening with Shagun at the wheel. Mahesh and Priti who also had several years of driving experience, decided to give free hand to Shagun to drive and curb their parental tendency to keep correcting her every now and then which can be very disturbing for the driver.

Shagun started driving that day, did not display any signs of nervousness and took off confidently. However, on the way she was shouting at every vehicle which was passing by, cursing them for overtaking their car as well as shouting at every other driver who would have to brake suddenly. Finally, Mahesh was forced to tell her to mind her behaviour and not hurl abuses at every other passer by.

It so emerged that she was her over-confident self who was required to improve on her temperament to be able to drive in a stable manner. Finally, they reached the friend's place and the parents and the special sister heaved a sigh of relief. Later, back home, Priti mentioned to Mahesh "She will have to be in control of her mannerisms while she is driving, otherwise she will land herself and us in a mess. While driving, one has to be conscious of moving vehicles and your own to avoid any risk of damage to any car or the occupants."

Mahesh replied "I fully understand and appreciate, your concern, your highness! The good part is that she is her usual confident self which is a desirable trait when it comes to driving abilities. Most learners are apprehensive and nervous. She is not! I will have to regularly communicate with her to mellow down while driving and be in control but keep her wavered temperament out of her mind, at that time."

The extent of the impact on account of Shagun was immense on the parents and sister, as narrated in detail in various areas of this book, so far. The parental involvement in matters relating to her was unavoidable as they were all living together as a family. There is very clearly a substantial difference in mindsets of the parents vis-à-vis Shagun, a youngster representing a product of today's generation, while it can be said that one reason could be immaturity because of young age, the cynicism, the abruptness and behavioural anomalies are quite unexplainable and can best be attributed to the fast changes in thought processes, with the passage of time.

The family continues to grapple with their matters as highlighted, time and again, in this chapter and earlier. Shagun's food habits, as talked about earlier, though briefly, is a pointer to the addiction which the young generation, needs to pause and think as to why, junk food which used to be earlier consumed for a change, are a regular part of a youngster's daily life and in the process, regular veg and non veg food, is no longer a preferred option. Shagun, too, would be frequently seen having wafers, with a burger along with a cold drink to wash it down. Ther are various types of healthier continental dishes with a tremendous variety, but not to her liking.

Today, the world over, there are cooking shows where actually delightful dishes are made out of amazing recipes. Likewise, laptops and mobiles have flooded the world with vastly improved models connecting people with the rest of the world. However, it is unexplainable as far as the extent of their usage which can be a huge hindrance if clung to, beyond limits.

There is no doubt that they are fantastic socially connecting mediums but the extent of addiction to them whether it is night or day is not justified.

In the instant case, Shagun is not using it for professional betterment but is content to be socially connected, that too, in the wee hours of the morning, disrupting her own office routine by leaving home when half the day is over. The meal timings are also untimely as her breakfast is at lunchtime and is content with an odd snack at teatime and then dinner at her pace, late in the night.

Let us now move forward to the remaining chapters of this book. So far, the emphasis has been on the relationship between a set of parents and a young daughter, Shagun and her special younger sister, Kiran. The focal point has been Shagun and her unusual habits, behaviour while tracing the route from the time when she used to be a small smiling kid who would attract everybody around her with her sweet captivating smile and who was extremely quick in estabilishing a bond with everyone she met.

As time passed, the situation changed and she grew up nursing grudges against her parents, developing a outrageous behaviour with them, and undesirable habits and a short tempered nature. It was a indeed a challenging situation for the parents who felt a sense of responsibility to try and change the situation for the better. their concern for both their children for the difficult future ahead has been highlighted. A host of situations were described along with the parents sharing their innermost feelings about their individual assessments as well as the need to desperately change the tide in favour of peace and harmony in their house.

The next chapter is focussed on yet another dimension of Shagun's life and the related repercussions faced by her and the family. The book is at the ultimate stage and focusses on the manner in which the parents win over the confidence of their elder daughter, Shagun and how the scenario changes in the house through the strategy of "self change"

Before we get onto that stage, let us see and draw our own inferences on the setback to Shagun and her ongoing relationship with her boyfriend.

Chapter 9

"A friendship that Went Sour"

It is an age old belief that excess of everything is undesirable and does not lead to positive results. We need to not only understand this but apply it in our lives. The same is true when it is seen in the context of relationships. This would apply to married lives of a happy couple. The more often the respective spouses see each other, the greater is the likelihood of differences cropping up between them. To elaborate further, Priti sees her husband in the mornings and late evenings culminating in deep slumber in the night. Alternatively, if she were to see him for greater durations in the house there would be a greater probability of interactions resulting in arguments.

Shagun is now 24 yrs of age and is steadily improving in her career. Her relationship with her parents continues to be on tenterhooks all the time. In the previous 2-3 yrs the frequency of her meeting him had become 2-3 times a week. She used to be either in the house or out with him.

Ideally, the parents could have put their foot down, but that would have only worsened the situation. The times of pinning down children, not giving them their space was not acceptable to children, the world over. Parents do learn their lessons, too, and prefer to coexist peacefully. Kiran had also grown up and her level of perception had improved considerably, though she was way behind in basics of academics. She now freely moves around the house, bending her knees, and falls, at times, due to imbalance. Due to friction in surfaces outside, she is invariably held by the hand and she walks but not for long distances. Any appreciation she gets, thrills her specially if there is some sense of achievement involved. Nevertheless, special children do miss out on a complete and normal childhood. Realising this, Shagun included, would get her gifts, at the drop of a hat! Priti was talking to Mahesh one day "Kiran, though lagging far behind, is more balanced in her actions than Shagun and acts more responsibly. Shagun, on the other hand, is bound to invite trouble, considering the frequency with which she is meeting her boyfriend, with whom she has a relationship for the last 3-4 yrs now. What do we do?" Mahesh shrugged his shoulders! "What can we do? Much as I would like to restrain you know what will happen! I am at my wits' end. We have crossed the stage of repeated counselling, and like most parents are clueless!"

That evening too she was out with him for dinner. She came back at midnight. Earlier, the parents had on innumerous occasions tried to explain to her the necessity of coming back on time. Her standard reply was "I can handle things and have faith on me" Priti once told her "We trust you completely. That is not the issue! There has to be a time frame to such outings. What is wrong in this? We are not stopping you from meeting him!" However, there was something amiss that night as Shagun was muttering something to her self as she entered the house and banged the door of her room. Priti went scampering after her and started knocking on the entrance door. The reply was abrupt and crisp "I am fine, go away from here!" Priti walked to her room and woke up Mahesh who was fast asleep. She told him "Something has happened. She came in uttering some gibberish and banged her room door not even bothering that Kiran was already asleep there, in her room. Do you want to talk to her now?" Mahesh said "Do not panic! She must have had a tussle with him. Lets talk to her tomorrow. You also should not feel pressurised and sleep now."

Priti could not sleep for some time thinking about Shagun and her predicament, post her dinner with her boyfriend the previous night. She knew that in the morning rush for office, Mahesh would not be able to talk to her. So, she decided to talk to Shagun the moment she got up in the morning. Finally, she was able to sleep. The next day morning started the usual way with Kiran being readied to go to school and Mahesh to office. Surprisingly, Mahesh did not discuss the problem and just told her not to worry and left for the day. Priti did not want Kiran to be around when she spoke to Shagun about the supposed fracas the previous night. Finally, it was noon when Shagun got up and came out of her room to have a cup of tea.

Promptly, she said "I need to talk to you. What happened yesterday?" Shagun responded immediately "Mom this is my personal problem and it would be better for you to concentrate on your house hold chores rather than quizzing me."

Priti this time was stern and said "You are used to talking to me this way for the last several years and keep reminding me that I am only a house maker. I am proud to be one. But that does not mean that you can do your thing and operate independently, while continuing to stay in this house. You are a part of a family and we are one of the few genuine wellwishers you have in this big bad selfish world." Shagun paused and said "His qualifications are good enough and he is on wellpaying job and so am I, settled, though in a different capacity being self employed. It had been discussed and mutually agreed that we should now get married and lead a life together.

He has changed his decision completely and now wants to do a three yr course in marketing and sales management. I was surprised and asked him why he is oscillating in his decision making? He curtly replied that it is a matter of his professional betterment and that if it did not suit her, they could part ways."

Priti replied "What you said was correct but you did not ask him how he could suggest parting of ways so casually after courting her for 3-4 years?" Shagun said "I did! In response he said that situations do change and cannot be assumed to remain the same and there can be always rethinking on any matter. I was dazed! I asked him whether there was any other reason to which he said that three years is not a long time and surely she could spend that time on making her business grow. He would be away for just three years and she should wait for him."

Priti said "What do you want to do? We have not met him as you did not let us do so, so we cannot comment on what is the right course of action for you now." Shagun shrugged her shoulders and said "I am confused! Lets also talk to papa and see what he has to say." Priti smiled "Now you are talking like a sensible girl who wants to have a balanced view on the issue, unlike innumerous occasions earlier when you simply dismissed what we had to say. Always remember that in the event of any matter you will always find us there for you!"

Mahesh returned from office, refreshed himself and sat in the living room, understanding the sombre look on the faces of both Priti and Shagun, barring Kiran who was up and about and telling him about her school and what happened that day in her characteristic broken unclear language which was steadily improving with speech therapy. Mahesh asked Priti "So, how was the day? And looked towards Shagun as well. All well?" Priti responded "I have been talking to her the whole day about what happened the previous night."

He expressed his astonishment "Well, this is a rarity! Mother and daughter communicating with each other. We must thank Shagun for not telling her mother to mind her own ways and not meddle in hers'. She has a poor impression of you as you are not a working person." Shagun finally retorted "Papa, do not enrage me by saying all this! If you do not want to talk properly, then I can get up and go."

It was Mahesh's turn to rebuke her "Despite all our efforts, in the preceding years you never allowed us to even engage you in a conversation, let alone help as parents. You had got carried away with yr success as a self employed and instead of humbling down. You were affront with us all the time. Priti must have told you, as earlier, that we are the few who will even discuss yr problems and suggest solutions, your friends will never be able to do so and can only help till a point."

Shagun, for the first time in several years, said "Papa, I am sorry,!" And started crying, something which she had never done earlier as she was her usual confident self. Priti's eyes were also misty. The situation required Mahesh to comfort his family rather than talking about earlier issues. He told Shagun "Do not worry at all, we will collectively arrive at a solution. Cool down, both of you!" Priti then went on to explain to him what had happened.

Mahesh then asked Shagun "Tell me, are you in love with him or are you not?" Shagun replied "We have been good friends, nothing more than that! We used to like meeting each other and do enjoy each other's company. That's all." Mahesh paused and said "Test him! Tell him that lets keep it open for the next three years ie the duration of the course, without any sense of commitment to each other in terms of marriage.

Let him not feel that you are head over heels, in love with him. By doing so, you will be taking him by surprise and also be able to guage his reactions. Stop calling or meeting him! Do not misunderstand me!

This would be a strategy on your part to know whether he is serious about this relationship with you. We are not trying to ask you to breakoff from him. However, you should be sure of his intentions. Time will prove that for you." Priti was exhilarated! She exclaimed "Mahesh this is brilliant! Shagun, I am sure that you would agree with him. Marriage is a serious affair. You should be 100% sure about each other's emotions before entering into a bond."

Shagun had received an emotional setback in life and was not prepared to face it without any moral support than from noneother than her own parents. It took this disruptive influence in her life to open the path for her parents to restart a bonding with her family. Shagun agreed to her father's suggestion and acted on it.

Later, Mahesh told Priti "This is a glorious opportunity for us to turn things around and, over time, estabilish a bond with her which should be strong and indestructible for all times to come. This is good for us as well as for Kiran who will understand human values better, seeing peace and harmony in our house after a long and strenuous time." Priti was also happy and relieved to be also able to strike a chord with her daughter, as a mother.

Time passed and one day Shagun's boyfriend expressed a desire to have dinner with Shagun. She promptly called her mother to convey the same to her. Priti promptly called Mahesh and asked him as to what has to be done. Mahesh thought about it and called her back to communicate to her that Shagun should refuse and not meet him. Priti quickly told Shagun who, in turn acted on the parental advice. It was with great difficulty that Shagun managed to convince her friend that she was busy and could not meet him. Then, one fine day Priti got a call from Shagun's friend pleading with her to ask her to take his calls.

Priti immediately rang up Mahesh to tell him accordingly. Mahesh reacted "He is getting desperate! Tell him if he calls up again that Shagun is not keen on talking to him." Priti did just that when he called again. The guy was obviously baffled at not being able to figure out what had happened. Shagun was also enjoying the developments. The guy, logically speaking, was missing her company. On her parents' advice, Shagun finally gave a call to him enquiring about his welfare. He finally asked her "Do you want to cut off from me? You have not been taking my calls." Shagun retorted "You have betrayed my trust! We had earlier discussed in detail, thought and finally came to a decision that we are, by and large settled and we should now tie the knot. What happened suddenly?" he replied that he was not prepared for marriage and wanted to improve upon his professional qualifications. Shagun then gave a crisp reply "You cannot take me for granted! So, now, we will keep our options open! You can do your management course ad lets see how we stand then, at that point of time. There is no commitment either ways!"

Later, Priti explained to Shagun why it is necessary to maintain that necessary distance while dating the more you keep meeting each other, the tendency is to take each other for granted. Priti said "Yr father had tried to explain so many times but yr reaction put us off so badly that we thought time is a big player and you would sooner or later realise you mistake." Shagun replied apologetically "I thought I knew him so well and was shocked to hear what he had to say after we had taken a conscious decision to get married and I was on the verge of informing you also"

Priti continued "Do you realise how you had been interacting with your parents all these years! Not once did you feel that your behaviour was crazy, illogical? You have been treating me as dirt just because I am not a working person! Who would have taken care of Kiran when you know that I have to attend to her primary functions also! Do you know of any mother who has to do this beyond a certain age of normal healthy children?"

Shagun started crying saying "I am extremely sorry, mom, I was in a arrogant world of my own! I had no realisation what I was doing?" Priti promptly got up and hugged her feeling emotional about the situation and said "Better late than never! Your father and me have spent endless days figuring out why you were affront with us and what we needed to do to mend the situation. Kiran is also growing and is sensible enough to understand that all was not well in our relationship as parents, with you. This was having a negative effect on her which we could see but you were lost in a world of yr own., to even understand this! You must apologise to yr father also. Remember come hell or high water, we are always there for you, keeping yr welfare in our minds."

It actually required a jolt in Shagun's life to jerk her to open her eyes to the realities of life and comprehend the significance of her parents in her life. In such situations, the moral support in any adverse circumstance is vitally important for all of us. The support mechanism provided by ones' own family represents a bond which is the strongest. This reality is a factor which is fast getting eroded from the mindsets of youngsters.

The need may vary from time to time but the support of parents is always there. Likewise, parents when old in age need emotional support as well, which must be reciprocated as well by the children. The world is changing but it is vital for us to ensure that humanistic values should not be eradicated from the minds and of all individuals.

That evening when Mahesh returned from office he could sense a feeling of buoyance on Priti's face, while Kiran was actually playing with Shagun. He immediately felt a sense of divine relief throughout his entire being. On seeing her father, Shagun surprisingly got up to give a glass of water to him, much to the surprise and astonishment of Priti who was standing closeby. Shagun broke into tears again and hugged her father. Mahesh was dumbstruck at this but thoroughly pleased as well as he could immediately understand Shagun's reactions. Shagun said "Papa please forgive me for mis-behaving with you for years! I have woken up now! Infact, I have already made up with mom! I am sorry to Kiran as well!"

Mahesh smiled "Shagun do not worry at all! We are there for you, let us get back to old times when we used to be a close knit family! Its been ages!" Later, Mahesh spoke to Priti "This is a blessing in disguise! Lets us now inculcate the principle of" self change "In all aspects of our lives to mend our relationships within the family. That is the only way to improve our wellbeing and estabilish an indestructible bond with both our daughters." Priti was in tears as well and said "I have been yearning for peace and harmony in our lives while wondering whether that would ever be possible. This is like a dream comig true." Mahesh said "This is a passing phase of Shagun's life! Lets consolidate our respective positions, as parents. You develop yr independent equation as a parent. We will keep doing so collectively as well."

Kiran, too, was upbeat seeing harmony all around. Shagun had also realised what her parents had been, all along, supportive to her. When she was now in a jam as she was vis-à-vis her boyfriend, it was her parents who had helped all along and told her the right course of action. With the recent developments, her sense of ego, arrogance had melted away. However, she was not depressed over the break up with her friend, but she was no longer her usual over confident self.

In the morning of the next day, Priti asked Shagun what she would like to have for dinner when the entire family was together. Shagun promptly replied "Spanish omelette and chicken mayonesse! You make it very well." Priti was thrilled! So was Mahesh! Things were improving! That day Mahesh was nice and well mannered with all in office. He also realised that while implementing self change, all the fingers point at your own self and you cannot hold anybody responsible for your agonies.

Through self change, we take it upon ourselves to improve our situation by identifying those areas of our personality which require to be improved upon and actually try to do so. He told Priti to do the same and both actually felt the external environment also responded for the better. Priti told Mahesh "I am now trying to be nice with the maids as well, while using my mind at the same time, so that they do not take advantage of the situation." Mahesh responded "Spot on! This is what we need to do! With immediate effect lets try and apply it in our daily lives and reap the benefits! We will oly be happier."

Hence, both of them embarked on the path of self change applying it every minute of their daily lives with their children and the whole world. Mahesh started talking politely to the peon of the office and started handling tough problems with calm and ease, rather than in a state of acrimony and panic. The interactions with the customers / suppliers also improved with the day passing by happily despite being confronted with complex issues. Similarly, Priti was having a better time, managing the domestic issues with calm and comfort.

Shagun interpreted the fracas with her friend as an affront to her self pride and prestige. This was the prime reason that she had mellowed down considerably and was more aligned with her family rather than going by her own rigid thought process, as earlier. This spelt a new lease of life to the family who had been thirsting for peace, well being and harmony.

Kiran, too, was upbeat as she was able to discern the change of atmosphere and was understandably pleased seeing her smiling parents as well. Priti mentioned to Mahesh "Why don't you talk to Shagun about her work as well try and figure out how it is faring and whether she would like to continue being on her own or consider doing a well-paying job which she deserves based on her qualifications and rich exposure in the industry."

Mahesh was a little circumspect in talking to her about her profession as she had snubbed him publicly regarding his quizzing her about her work. This was because she always felt that she was the only one responsible for her growth and she was good at her work and that is why she was able to impress clients and get the projects.

To a considerable extent, she was right in thinking this way but all of us know there is a supreme force which is helping us in achieving our objectives and that is a realisation which does not easily register on youngsters' minds. Nevertheless, Mahesh decided to choose the right time to talk to Shagun and understand her work profile and help her if necessary. So, one Sunday when they were all relaxing in the house when he decided to talk to her.

Mahesh started the communication "How is yr work getting along? Would you like to discuss it over." Pat came the reply from the Shagun they had been used to over the years, "Papa, I am going through a personal problem but that does not give you the right to interfere with my office where you have no role to play.!"

Papa was taken aback by the abruptness of the reply but was determined to keep showing the change in himself. As was earlier discussed with Priti, he paused and thought that he must soothen her nerves and said "I will never intrude in your work arena but let me remind you that you did need help in a personal matter and you will agree that we did not interfere but helped you in handling the same. As of now, I know very little about yr work but let me caution you that in case of a problem, I may not be able to help you even if I want to because of the nature of the problem which may be vastly different from a relationship hassle which you faced now."

Shagun suddenly got up and went to her room. Priti and Kiran were looking serious while Mahesh was smiling. Priti quizzed Mahesh "For heaven's sake, do not smile, if Shagun sees you like this she would misunderstand you for grinning at her. What you said was correct but the resulting smile is unjustified!" Mahesh owed her a reply "Remember we were discussing the other day about "self change".

I am just applying it using my common sense which we need to do all the time to successfully show the difference in us to people, even though it may be yr own family. I will be doing the same with you and Kiran as well. Just wait and see!" Priti by now was all smiles and said "I think you are right! I will do the same. But while doing so, I will be careful and use my common sense as well so that I do not let the situation boomerang back at me."

It was now Kiran's turn now to say something and she obliged "Papa and mom, I copy you both to see what to happen." In her broken language, Kiran managed to convey what she had to say while also accorded her esteemed consent to what her parents were discussing, fully understanding everything. Shagun, on the other hand, was her arrogant self though she had received a setback on the personal front. Nobody can bring about a sea change in one's own self overnight.

That also does not mean that Shagun would have to go through a series of jolts to set her negativities in order. The parents, in this situation have seen some hope in mending the relationship with their daughter through her breakup with her boyfriend. Hence, the breakup was an opportunity to reestabilish the emotional bond with their daughter, and a golden one at that!

Next day was a usual working day and Mahesh reached office on time. The industrial environment was not too positive and hence Mahesh and his partner had to be careful in striking a balance between stock and collectibles from customers ie payments to be collected. There was immense pressure from the suppliers to place orders on them for further supplies, with stock already piled up.

On reaching office he was innundated with calls for placement of orders. He politely explained to the principals that this was a difficult period and they needed all their support from them to manage the situation. Mahesh contacted all their dealers to assess if they would be keen on, in turn, placing any orders on them.

The system used to work in this format as Mahesh's company had a dealer network who used to, from time to time, place orders on them and their company used to interact and place supply orders on the principals, for supplies. That day, apparently there was a high level meeting at the principals' head office wherein it emerged that the factories had exceeded production targets and were flooded with stock of all varieties of groceries and toiletries. Hence, it was a management decision to pressurise the distributors like Mahesh's company, to place further orders so that they could clear their stocks in the factories.

Anticipating the pattern of demand in the coming months Mahesh's company was constrained to place lumpsum orders on their principals, on the basis of loaned funds from bankers. The repercussions were that the dealers, would have to, in turn, bail out the distributor, to stock more and sell more. Mahesh and his partner were also required to be on their toes to keep track of their stock position as well as payments. In all the melee, while Mahesh's partner was panicking, Mahesh was for the first time taking considered action to control the situation rather than blowing his top at his subordinates.

It is commonly observed that under work pressure bosses in office are known to transmit the pressure on to the colleagues and subordinates who, for obvious reasons have to digest the fluctuating tempers of their superiors. Mahesh, also, till recently was one of the many typical superiors across the globe.

However, in a desperate bid to lead better lives he decided to enforce "self change" using his common sense all the time. This was based on various religious teachings wherein it was stated that we can be in control of our destiny through a genuine effort on our part to first identify those areas of our inner selves which require change for the better. The more we exert ourselves in this direction, the more will be the visible change all around us. We will exercise more discipline and be in control of situations rather than let situations control us.

On that eventful day in office, everybody was talking more about Mahesh's temperament rather than the problem on hand. They were surprised to notice that Mahesh was coolheadedly handling the various issues without getting bogged down by them.

On the other hand Mahesh's partner was panicstricken and blowing his top at the staff. In the midst of this he also noticed that Mahesh was not looking perturbed at all and was upfront facing the situation. He was trying his best to control the scenario. He could not resist asking Mahesh "How come you are so cool? These guys in our office do not work at all and we are having to face all the pressure. I will have to have a couple of drinks in the night to be able to sleep properly."

Mahesh responded "Look, panicking does not help nor does transferring the blame to others! As partners who are managing the show, we are the ones who have to spearhead the bowling attack in cricketing terms. Hence, we have to tackle the problems to the best of our abilities." The partner looked at him completely nonplussed and dumbfounded! He asked him to explain to him in detail some other time, as his mind was too cluttered at that time. Finally, with the orders placed, the principals also calmed down and assured them that they would extend all help to them if Mahesh's coy is not able to liquidate the excess stock in a reasonable amount of time.

Mahesh came back home and entered the house with a smile on his face which was invariably not the case, in recent as well as distant times. Seeing this, Priti could not resist asking "Mahesh, what is the matter? Did you have no work in office today? How come you look so elated?" Mahesh excitedly told her "It is all the magic of self-change. I have started applying it in office as well. Priti, it works in any situation! Today, was perhaps, was one of the most stressful days in recent times. Yet I managed to weather the storm!"

Shagun who too had just returned from office also chose to ask her papa "What happened? But, you do not look pressurised! You look relieved instead. What is the trick, papa?" Mahesh replied quickly "I will explain to you one day! Right now you must be tired." Shagun said "Okay, papa, tell me tomorrow! Ok?" Mahesh replied in the affirmative.

Later, Mahesh explained to Priti what had happened in office. "I was more pleased with the staff's reaction to my temperament rather then the problem itself which I was anyways grappling with. I was thrilled in making people see the change in me. I will definitely take this process forward."

Priti replied "Actually, I am feeling the same way. Rather than cribbing about life's problems it is more important to fight them keeping our self change method in place. Our neighbours were also pleasantly surprised at my talk. Actually, while we have been able to understand the essence of self change by way of a deep introspection, not everyone would like or accept faults with his or her own self. It is a lot easier to point fingers at others for their own problems. This leads further to self pity and grudging our own existence."

Mahesh replied "You are absolutely right! But that is the only way to lead a better life and be in control of the situation. People must have the urge and willpower to try and genuinely try to improve thir lot." Priti went on "We are lucky that we are able to embark on this path and achieve progress in this direction. We must be thankful to the almighty for this positive realisation, and also you too for understanding this from religious teachings and imbibe it correctly." Mahesh responded "I had read this in various teachings various times but did not understand how to implement it. I read it only some time back that while god exists in all human beings, it is through improving our weak areas that we can improve our wellbeing, and ie to change ourselves."

A couple of days later Shagun asked Mahesh about the tension that had gripped his office, as described earlier to which Mahesh decided to narrate the entire instance to her so that she could draw a parallel with situations in her office, though he was unaware about her office work culture.

In response, Shagun surprised her father by seeking his advice in a matter concerning her office, something she had never done before. Priti who was also sitting there, was pleasantly surprised. So was Kiran who on hearing her sister decided to ask her in her characteristic broken language "You say papa not know anything, what now happened?"

Shagun was speechless on hearing this and simply asked her to keep quiet. She went on to tell her father about the problem she told him about a wealthy customer who approached her, held a meeting with her and her associates about a project which involved opening a retail outlet selling all types of fashion garments.

Shagun showed him their catalogue with different designs to select from as well as for accessories as well. He reposed full confidence in Shagun's abilities and approved various designs and confirmed the sizes and the quantities as well. He paid a substantial advance as well but also said that he travels a lot and that they could be in contact on the net. Shagun and her team, thrilled with bagging this order.

Having bagged the order, their entire team had dinner together and chalked out the strategy of the artwork to be done and the other functions as sourcing the cloth and so on. Shagun said "Papa, everything was going smoothly and I did my best in preparing the artworks so that when seen on garments they would simply look spectacular. We also had the future potential in mind while proceeding with the execution of the order. I was in constant touch with him and when I asked him to approve the artworks on the mail, he said he was travelling and really did not have the time to focus on the artworks. He further said that he had complete faith in my abilities."

Mahesh interrupted and asked "Did you make him realise the significance of the artworks based on which only you will be proceeding with the execution of the order.?" Shagun replied "Papa, he was sounding very busy on the phone also and was hardly responding to the updates we were mailing to him regularly. He did not give his written approval to the artworks or a mail to this effect!"

Mahesh continued "That is where you erred in not insisting on an approval on the same because the approval of the designs forms the very basis of the execution of the order. His intentions were genuine and he did repose full trust in you and your team. But, Shagun, procedures and systems must be strictly followed. Then, what happened?" She continued "He did tell me repeatedly that I should continue with the processing of the order and that I had his approval.

Based on this understanding, he continued with his part of remitting further payments and held the last instalment which he was required to pay after receiving the finished garments. So, we went ahead and did our very best in completing the entire range of garments in the exact quantities he had ordered." It was now Mahesh's turn to quiz her further, as the discussion was coming to its final stage.

He asked "Were your garments in exact accordance with the designs?" Shagun replied "Yes, papa, I made doubly sure that we don't falter anywhere because we wanted further orders from him. The entire consignment was neatly packed and despatched to him at the desired location.

His reaction on examining the garments was a complete anti-climax! He rang me up expressing his disappointment on the majority of the garments. He said they were good but not to his liking! I was in tears! I told him that we are regularly getting such orders and he was aware of that fact. However, he insisted that if nothing could be done now, he would return the rejected garments and pay only for the ones he had accepted. I argued with him trying to make him realise that she was not at fault!

However, he did not pay the remaining instalment, but returned the rejections back to us. The margin of profit we had envisaged got reduced although we ended up making a neat profit. But, it did not end nicely and he has, so far, not contacted us again, for further requirements."

Mahesh clearly saw the lack of experience on the part of Shagun and her team whereby they did not plug the loopholes which had resulted in this situation. However, he did not want to bogg her down due to this occurrence, and calmly told her "Look, by and large, you did what you should have done! Nevertheless, you should have politely insisted on getting a written approval of the artworks, explaining the possible problem which can ensue and actually happened in terms of his rejections.

"Always remember while sending the finished garments to the customers, at the final stage, route the despatch documents through your bankers to ensure that the bank gets the payment and then releases the consignment to the customer. That bank would then remit the payment to your bankers and you will be able to secure your payment."

Shagun looked embarassed and replied "Papa, I was not aware of this system and would ensure that we follow it in future. Thanks for telling me, papa" It was now time for Priti to chip in and said "You will now be able to understand that you need to discuss your office affairs with, at least, your father! Do you think your father will ever give you incorrect advice? There are certain things we all learn over time.

However, to the extent yr father knows out of his experience, he will definitely tell you. The other alternative is that over time you will learn anyways!" Shagun also realised that due to unnecessary ego and a misguided sense of arrogance, she refused to involve her parents in her official matters, which, as she now realised was a fundamental mistake on her part. Kiran also had to make a statement. So she said "Talk office with papa! He is the best papa!" Shagun this time gave her a hug instead of asking her to keep quiet.

The situation was undoubtedly improving in their house hold. Shagun had started calling in office to seek clarifications on a routine basis. The sense of self pride and arrogance had been replaced by good and clean thinking. The frequency of arguments had gradually come down and Shagun was now going to the other extreme by talking about office with her father during dinner as well.

Priti was on the verge of correcting her when Mahesh talked to her and restricted her from doing so. He said "Priti, let her talk her heart out! This will only strengthen our lack of bonding with her which was solely responsible for disharmony. Moreover, remember, we have to continue with our strategy of self change! The more, the better! Let her also ponder and think and figure out why we are also not rebuking her or not even correcting her. She must see the change in both of us!"

Priti understand Mahesh's point and decided to do her bit in furthering this bonding with Shagun. Priti, therefore, made conscious to efforts do polite talk with her elder daughter constantly asking her about what she wanted to have for supper or whether she wanted to go shopping, once a while, being careful about not making it a regular feature as she was well aware that Priti bought well known branded clothes only which were far more expensive from relative lesser known brands. Shagun was also sensitive to the changes in the interaction of her parents and was talking about the same to her friends.

Shagun was having a get-together with her friends one day, in the evening and had told Priti well in advance. They used to have such get togethers once in a month when they would exchange notes on the experiences of the month. This time, however, Shagun unlike others was not being critical of her parents but was curious of whether her friends were aware of what was "self change" all about!

In response, one of her friends did mention that it was a process of changing our own inner selves, holding ourselves responsible for all our negativities and make a genuine effort to change our circumstances through our own efforts. Hearing this, Shagun was pacified as she was under the impression that her parents were evolving a strategy to control her and was, in the process, confused, as they were actually helping her to the extent possible.

However, he did ask her friend "How on earth can you hold yourself responsible for yr own negative occurences? They are pre-destined! God's desire for who has to suffer and who does not have to!" The friend replied "Look, whatever is predetermined in my life is a result of my karmic acts of previous lifetimes, not yours! Hence, I can be only responsible for my acts of the past. Shagun, what is so difficult to understand in this?"

Shagun did not have the depth of mind to comprehend this understanding! However, her friend had correctly understood the essence! Shagun's mind was too clustered and clouded with her own achievements, for her to grasp this reality. Her friend continued "This understanding leads to a better quality of life and one does not easily get flustered due to adverse circumstances while the positive occurences are anyway taken for granted! It can be applied to every minute of our day to day life. I am already applying it and felt positive energy in me and around me.! You should all try to do the same!" The group of friends at Shagun's place were dazed with what she had to say! One of them remarked that they are too young to do all this and maybe when they are old they should attempt to try and implement this in their lives.

Shagun, later was recapitulating on what that friend had to say and it seemed to impact her, also because there was positivity in her house ever since she heard her parents talk about it. She thought that she has to apply it in her daily life and is not required to go for any lecture to anybody's house. Suddenly, she decided to apply it in her daily routine, in the house, in transit and at office as well.

Before embarking on it she decided to meet that friend of her's to know what precisely she was doing in her daily life. She soon contacted her and fixed a time the very next day in the evening at her place as she did not want Mahesh and Priti to know about it at this stage. Priti, on hearing about it remarked "Shagun you just met her two days back! What has happened?" Shagun replied "Mom, it is concerning one of her projects and it is urgent!" Priti was still not convinced but decided not to probe further, lest it would invoke an unnecessary reaction, from her. She was keen on taking the process of self change forward, as discussed with Mahesh, time and again. She told Shagun "No hassles! Shagun, I was merely inquiring! Pl go ahead and do not make it too late!" "Ok, mom" replied Shagun.

Shagun had already noticed a positive change in this friend of hers' and was keen on asking her pointed questions which were specific! So, she reached her friend's place in the evening on the next day and had a detailed talk with her. She quizzed "To start with, how did you come to know about this?" The friend replied "My mother explained to me and she managed to convince me how I would be able to change my life with the overhauling of my mindset.

She went ahead and said "Shagun, first I mended my behaviour in the house with my family as I was very self centred and thought only of myself. I immediately saw a change in all of them in the house towards me. Then onwards, I used to walk out of the house for work with a positive frame of mind. There after, I used to exercise self control in the office, despite all provocations. I visibly saw a distinct change in the attitude of all my colleagues towards me. In fact, it was very pleasing to note that they were desperate to know why I am not getting into vicious arguements like before, and how she had mellowed down so much."

Shagun then asked her "How did you benefit from this apart from just feeling good?" The friend replied "Shagun, you are viewing this from the monetary point of view only! You cannot interpret gains from just physical and tangible point of view! Even, to get financial benefits you must have the right mindset using your intelligence all the time. This is not possible if you are short tempered or egoistic or even an arrogant human being! Don't you agree?" "It was now Shagun's turn to elaborate "Yes I agree completely! If I look back I do realise how horribly I behaved with my family spread over several years. I would daily go out in a grumpy mood! The effect of this trait did clearly have an impact on the rest of the day and I would end the day not being happy."

The friend intervened "Remember, that if we behave miserably there would be an equal and opposite reaction over time, ie it is logical because if we do not behave ourselves other would only reciprocate the same in equal measure." Shagun was, by now convinced with what her friend had to say.

Shagun was convinced that this is a powerful thought process which can change the way we think. However, she was not clear whether one would have the courage to continue practising it, in day to day life, in the face of of adversity. She asked her friend "Have you tried it out in negative circumstances? How does it work? It is ok to feel happy in normal circumstances but the real test lies in being mentally strong in being in control of oneself, when one is prone to be carried away by the negativity of a circumstance!"

Shagun's friend saw the question coming and was ready for it "I know you well enough! I knew that you will seek clarifications on this point! Look, what happens when there is a negative situation in the house or the office or while interacting with people? We feel low and start sulking and start questioning our very existence! Don't we do this? Instead, if we are mentally in control of ourselves, we are able to handle problems better and control the situation rather than let the situation control us. For instance, I used to get irritated very fast and instead of confronting the situation I used to be busy being in a irritable mood. One day in the office, my boss was very upset because one of my colleagues was absent and her work was pending.

"Normally, I would not have been concerned and would have been busy finishing my work only. Instead, that day, I went upto my boss and told him that I will complete her work also in addition to mine, by the end of the day. He stared at me and said that I am not going to be paid extra for this additional work. I told him that I know but I will do it." Shagun remarked "But that is stupidity! Your boss will in future ask you to complete the work of any of your colleagues who is absent on any day! Will you keep doing this?" The friend replied "If necessary, I will do it!

Now I will explain to you how I got the benefits. By doing so, my boss would have a better impression of me and would rate me at a level higher than others! Hence, my chances of a raise in salary are much higher than others! Secondly, my colleague was profusely thanking me for doing her work. So, if one day I am absent she will step in and do my work. In the process, I made a good friend out of my colleague." Shagun was dazed! This was a perspective of life she could not fathom. Her friend had presented a different way of leading your own life and be in control of it. Finally, she thanked her for telling her things which had never struck her at all. This way of life was described in a variety of books of different religious teachings.

It was time to go back home and she thanked her once again and went home, thinking of what her friend had told her. Shagun was deeply impacted by what she had learnt and was determined to take the process forward by implementing it in her daily life, first in her house and simultaneously in her office as well. As a matter of surprise, she decided to keep it as a secret from her family and actually try to make them see the difference in her over time. In the process, she will be able to derive pleasure from the surprise and astonishment which would show on the faces of her parents. This, she now thought, was the least she could do to neutralise the adverse effect her mis-demeanour has had on the relationship with the family as well as the resulting bad atmosphere in the house, for several years now.

Shagun had awakened! Let us now proceed to the final chapter of this book which shows how the relationships within the family got mended and the demonstrative effect it can have on millions of such families, across the globe, enabling them to lead better lives.

Chapter 10

The Path to Success and Happiness

Kiran, the special one, was looking for her wristwatch which she could not find and sought the help of her mother, to locate it, in the room. It was getting late for school. Priti then had to put her foot down and told Kiran "You can look for your watch when you come back from school. You are getting late!" However, she knew as well as the others how possessive she was in keeping her things and would daily spend half an hour before sleeping to keep her things in place, without fail.

However, that morning, Shagun was asleep and Priti was particular to speak softly to ensure that she does not emit a shout asking all of them to shut up, as was a daily feature for the last several years, early in the morning. Shagun was actually awake and was keenly listening to what her mother and Kiran were doing. She then smiled to herself and decided that this was the right time for her to embark on the process of "Self-change" and its implementation. So, she promptly got up and told her mother that she would locate Kiran's watch, she hunted for the same, located it and handed it to her mother

Kiran, was courteous enough to thank her sister saying "Thank you, sis! And sorry for disturbing you!" Shagun, on hearing this, gave her a hug and a kiss on her cheek Priti was understandably dumbfounded! She was speechless! This was something that she could not have imagined! Her mindset had been negatively influenced with the passage of the last two decades that an act of this kind, that too from Shagun, early in the day, was too positive to expect.!

A trivial act of this kind had made the parents thirsting for change and positivity. So, she also thanked Shagun for her help in locating her sister's watch and apologised for waking her up. Shagun simply said "You are welcome!" Priti went out thrilled with this ocurrence and after dropping Kiran at school, was yearning to tell Mahesh about it. Mahesh too, was astonished! He said to Priti "Fantastic! If we do good, the environment will also respond in a positive manner. Lets keep up the good work and reap the benefits!"

Priti replied "Certainly! The better is the quality of our interaction with her, the closer will be the bonding. Even if she reacts adversely, let us pause at the spur of the moment, think and then react. We would be then using our minds, not our hearts"

The situation was undoubtedly improving in their house and the general atmosphere was that of positivity. One fine day Shagun came back home elated and as soon as she reached the house she rushed to the parents' room with Kiran scampering after her. Shagun was holding some carry-bags in her hand. Mahesh had just come back from office and was in the process of changing his clothes when Shagun barged in. Priti restrained her urge to tell Shagun to knock before entering but instead told her that she could leave the packages there and come after 10 mins.

Shagun and Kiran retraced their steps and stood ouside the room for a while. After 10 mins, Shagun asked whether they could now come in or not? Priti felt that something was amiss and there was every possibility of a heated argument, as had happened umpteen times before. Priti asked them to come in and found that Shagun had a broad grin on her place. She had bought a shirt for Mahesh, a dress for her mother and a dress for Kiran as well. The sizes were perfect as Shagun was already aware of them. Priti queried "Any occasion, Shagun? The garments are great! And costly as well!"

Shagun replied "There is no occasion!" Actually, she had implemented the application of the strategy of "self change" and had seen the effect of the same and experienced the resulting pleasure. She had a meeting of all her colleagues and instead of having a strictly official meeting she introduced coffee and biscuits as well. This was a welcome gesture on her part and was appreciated by all. Moreover, the manner in which she conducted the meeting was informal interspersed with a sense of humour as well.

This lightened the atmosphere and the exchange of views was more on a friendly note. Later, everybody thanked her for bringing about this change which served the purpose of motivating all concerned to give their very best at work. Shagun was thrilled on seeing the change in the office and decided to splurge a bit on shopping for her family and surprising them as well.

However, she was keen on keeping this process of change, a closely guarded secret. On the other hand, the parents were surprised at this sudden and unexpected display of love and affection, for no rhyme or reason, so, Priti quizzed her further and said "Shagun, have you bagged a big project? Why have you spent a sizeable amount for no particular reason?" Mahesh, too, asked "Do not hide anything! Obviously, something positive has happened that is why you are giving us gifts!"

Shagun finally had to give an answer and said "The day went off smoothly, the colleagues are doing their work fine, that is all!" The parents and Kiran decided to thank her and kept their respective gifts. Before going to sleep, Priti did mention to Mahesh "What do you make out of this? Has she made up with her earlier boyfriend or what else, as she has never ever done anything like this before!" Mahesh responded "I have no clue either! However, it is not her boyfriend! The look on her face was a different type of happiness which is similar to what we are experiencing after trying to change our lives through self change. There was a genuine look of peace and contentment on her face, which I, as a father have never seen earlier. Let us observe her in the coming days."

The next day Priti asked Shagun what she wanted to have for dinner, the only meal they used to have together. In response, Shagun said "Mom you make anything, it is tasty! I have started eating everything! You do not have to ask me every day! Why don't you make what you want to have? We will all have it!" Priti was dumbstruck! Shagun had never reacted like this before!

She was puzzled! Here she was trying to win her over and in response Shagun was doing the same! So she decided to make what she wanted to make from everyone's point of view and served it at dinnertime. Shagun was the first one to praise the food and sat with them on the dining table and discussed some office matter with her father "Mahesh was in for a surprise as well and so was Kiran! Kiran said "Sis, you have become a good girl!"

Shagun displayed a broad grin on hearing this and replied "Kiran, you just wait and see there is a lot in store for you." Just then, she got a call from an irate customer enquiring about the status of an existing order. She was apparently ruffled at a call so late in the evening and was on the verge of telling the customer to ring up in morning, in office. However, she checked herself and instead apologised to the caller and told her the exact true situation, assuring her that she would keep her posted on a daily basis till the time the order is executed.

In the end, it was the caller who was highly apologetic and thanked her for the feedback as well. Mahesh, on hearing the proceedings, was delighted and felt proud of the fact that his daughter was evolving! and was becoming a mature entrepreneur. Priti felt the same as she mentioned to Mahesh later "Shagun is changing fast very unlike her usual short-tempered self we have been used to over the last decades." Mahesh remarked "Since we are in the process of changing ourselves, the environment in the house, too, is responding favourably!"

Priti felt the same way! "Better late than never! Nothing like having a happy, cohesive family, despite the challenges posed by life from time to time." One of the two telephone lines had stopped working and was not operational. Priti heard Shagun lodging a complaint for the same, something which she herself was used to doing. She was pleasantly surprised yet again.!

Mahesh had extended an invitation to one of his cousins to come over for dinner, the following Saturday, with their entire family. Priti was understandably, busy with the arrangements for the party at their house, on the week=end. It was a Saturday evening when Priti was busy in the kitchen when Mahesh and Shagun came back from their respective offices. Shagun straightaway went to the kitchen and asked Priti if she could help her in anything.

This was the first time she had ever volunteered to help her mother in any way. While Priti was pleasantly surprised she told her that there was no need and that she would manage on her own and Shagun should relax as she had just come from office. Shagun replied "Helping you in the kitchen would help me in relaxing, as this is different from my daily routine" Priti then turned around and asked "Shagun, you are behaving a trifle differently for the last couple of days but positively. What is the reason?"

Shagun had a broad smile on her face and said "I want to make you my best friend! Is that possible?" Priti responded "Certainly! I want the same! To start with, lay the table and make the salad. This would be a help from a friend!" Shagun promptly obliged and then went to get ready for the party.

The guests came around 8pm, and Mahesh first offered his cousin a drink which he readily agreed to while the ladies relished a glass of white wine. Shagun, too, expressed her desire to have wine and her father quickly made one for her as well. The families enquired about each other's well being and soon Shagun was also asked about her work.

She responded "I am doing fine and I have a competent consultant who is also a friend, philosopher and guide, and does not charge me anything. I am in better control of things as I am constantly learning from him." One of the guests asked "Who is he?" Shagun promptly replied "Papa, who else?" All of them had a hearty laugh. All this while Shagun was assisting her mother in serving snacks, while Mahesh was giving her appreciative glances which the daughter was enjoying!

The party went off fine! Priti, however, could not resist asking Shagun the reason for the change in her which was very apparent. The daughter replied "I am just copying you both and feeling good about it.! Do not worry! I do not have any hidden agenda!" Priti remarked "Great! What has propelled you into copying your parents who till some back were useless for you in all respects! I am being just inquisitive!"

Shagun gave her a hug and went away, not allowing her mother to probe further. Kiran, too, perceptive to the change, remarked "Sis has become a good girl like me!" Priti planted a kiss on her cheek and told her to go to bed, as it was getting late. Mahesh was in the room relaxing and trying to guage the change which his daughter had brought about in her interactions. With the family as well as everybody else. Priti mentioned "You must be a content father, to be praised by yr daughter before everybody in a party?"

He replied "By all means, yes! Shagun praising me is no mean achievement! I am trying to figure out what is the cause of this sudden change in her mannerisms.!" "Same here! I did try and quiz her but she did give evasive replies! Lets not pressurise her and provoke her unnecessarily!" Mahesh agreed with her and preferred to wait and watch. Little did they realise that she was also trying genuinely to change her ways, through the same mechanism which they were deploying through a continuous inner change.

A couple of days later Shagun expressed a desire to have good Chinese food and that it is going to be a treat from her side. This time Mahesh confronted her and asked "Shagun, what is on? Have you made up with yr previous boyfriend? Have you got some big projects recently?" Shagun replied "Firstly, my relationship with that guy is over! Don't even mention about him! In case I see anybody else, I will let you know! Work is doing fine! There have been no new projects recently!" He still persisted "You were talking about my advice the other day in the party! I was quite surprised but happy! Did you genuinely mean what you said?"

Shagun, while enjoying the question and answer session, replied "Papa, yr advice regarding the customer who had not seen the artworks, was correct. Whatever else, you have been telling me are actually eye-openers for me. Therefore, it makes a lot of sense to accept my earlier mistakes whereby I never listened to you about anything. I chose to accept this before the guests as well. I am sure I must have made them happy as well. Lets now go for a good Chinese meal!"

They started changing their office clothes into party wear and were about to leave when Shagun made a terse remark about Priti's dress "Mom, what are you wearing? Wear something more casual!" All of a sudden, she saw a shocked look on Priti's face and decided to check herself and said "Mom, no hassles! If you are comfortable wearing the dress, that is more important! Ignore my remark" Priti was yet again amazed! What is she upto? Her remark was typical of her being critical as in the earlier years and suddenly she changed and nullified her remark!

Shagun had successfully managed to baffle her parents and was enjoying every moment of the look of astonishment on their faces, in the last of couple of days she had said and done things which they, as parents, were yearning to see. The fact that she checked her otherwise sarcastic comment on her mother's dress was out of tune with her general personna and difficult for the parents to accept and digest, at face value. It was an interesting situation wherein the entire family was individually and collectively trying to make each other happy, without letting the daughter know and vice-versa about the driving force ie inner transformation, in other words, self change.

Priti, on the other hand, had changed her mode of communication with everybody including the maids who came to the house to do respective jobs, being more humane in her communication. Mahesh did the same in the office and realised that he gained in every possible way. It should be a way of life for every individual, he thought and had started taking pride in being different from others! Shagun was doing the same without letting her parents know that all of them were sailing in the same boat as far as self change is concerned. The negative situations in the house and the office were handled with a lot of poise and dignity.

The feel good factor, prompted Priti to suggest to Mahesh one day that they should consolidate the gains in peace and harmony by planning a visit as a rejuvenated family somewhere where they had not been in the past. She suggested Thailand to Mahesh who immediately liked the idea and showed kiddish excitement in the process.

The next day Mahesh went to office and assessed the situation from the point of view of whether he could go on a week's leave and, if so, when he could do so. Having examined from all parameters. Accordingly, it so emerged that Mahesh and family would be able to make the proposed visit to Thailand, a week later, for ten days in all. Mahesh thought that it made a lot of sense to spend a total of ten days in Thailand as the airfare and the hotel stay would cost a sizeable amount anyway and it would be worth the while to make the best of it not just in terms of sight seeing or shopping but also strengthen the bonding within the family even further, for the future.

He rang up Priti and told her "Sweetheart, we are all set to go to Thailand within a week for a total stay of ten days. Let us spring a surprise on the children today at dinner time" "Perfect timing" was Priti's reply. Mahesh finally got back from office and also peeped in the children's room to ascertain whether Shagun had also returned from office or not! Both sisters were busy playing some game. Things were changing as it was a rare sight to see Shagun playing with Kiran or involving her in something constructive. He promptly went to his room and refreshed himself and was all set for dinner. Later, Priti came and said "Have you done the visa formalities? It may take more than a week!" Mahesh was grinning and said "Your husband is quite efficient and the papers have already been submitted. It should ideally take just a couple of days to get the visas." Together, they proceeded for dinner and asked the children to join in. At the dining table Mahesh decided to do a bit of play-acting and mantained a serious look on his face and looked busy in his dinner.

Priti kept glancing at at him waiting for the moment when he would make an announcement. Finally, it was Shagun who spoke "Papa, how was your day? You look disturbed and serious!" Papa responded "No . . . . everything is fine, just a little occupied as I have to leave for Thailand for ten days, within a week!" The daughter asked "Okay, Thailand! Vow! Are you going alone?" Papa replied "No three more are going with me!"

Shagun continued "Are you even remotely suggesting that we are those three who are accompanying you to Thailand?" Mahesh could now not control any further and started grinning. Hell broke loose! Shagun started dancing and Kiran was emitting cries of delight in her own characteristic way! Priti realised that it was 10pm and neighbours would start wondering what they were upto! She told the kids to mellow down and Shagun said "My god! I hardly have time to finish my pending projects!" Priti also realised that she had a lot to coordinate before finally leaving for Thailand. The family was all pepped up to go for the holiday, and this time more so because there was an uncanny calm in the family. However, the parents were looking forward to this refreshing change, which promised a friendly atmosphere within the family, devoid of friction, as was a usual practice in the past several years.

The next few days before their departure were packed with demanding odd jobs to be tied up and finally it was the day of departure for Phuket in Thailand. They had to first reach Bangkok and take a connecting flight to Phuket. They reached the airport well in time and boarded their flight and reached Bangkok in time. The chaos started thereafter when they hardly had any time to clear the immigration formalities and rush with Kiran on a wheelchair. The chaos which resulted was enough to drive the family crazy.

They were the last ones to finally board the flight to Phuket. The airport was small but lively with lot of passengers either departing after a holiday or equal numbers arriving for an exciting vacation. Phuket was an exciting place and fairly crowded, bearing a cosmopolitan look. The resort was beautiful with lush green gardens and a spacious apartment with big bedroom and a sprawling living room with a facility of sofa cum bed to meet the requirements of the children.

The holiday had started! The children were thrilled by their experience so far. There was a swimming pool in the midst of the lawns. The stay in Phuket was exciting and the family took a cruise and had a whale of a time on the ship. The beaches were neat and clean and it was a pleasure to enjoy the view there. The family was there for a total of three complete days.

On the second day, Priti remarked to Mahesh "Shagun seems to have forgotten about shopping! She is busy sightseeing! Surprising!" Mahesh replied "Let me check with her and see her reaction!" So he decided to go to the living room where the two sisters were watching tv late in the evening he queried Shagun "Lets go shopping tomorrow! There are a couple of specialised markets here, which I am sure, would be of your liking."

Shagun appeared disinterested for a change and remarked "Papa, I do not think that I need anything. Moreover, it will be boring for you all!" Mahesh was surprised and continued "No harm in having a look! Maybe I may also find something worth my while! Lets try it out!" Shagun responded "Ok, if you insist!" Mahesh walked back to his room, while Shagun was grinning to herself!

She realised that a wee bit of self control and introspection changed the situation to such an extent that her father, for the first time ever, turned around and asked her if she wanted to go for shopping or not. Moreover, she also realised that there was no argument in the communication. She experienced a strange happy feeling which had the effect of boosting her self confidence.

Shagun was undoubtedly evolving and maturing into a thinking person. She decided to test the process of self improvement further in all nuances of daily life. In any case the family readied themselves to go to the shopping street. Priti and Shagun along with Kiran were simply dazed to see the variety of garments for men and women at affordable prices. Shagun, despite being apparently dazed at the range was restraining herself, from cutting loose and going on a shopping spree.

Mahesh could clearly see that and kept wondering what the matter was! He finally approached her and said "I can give you some money, so feel free to shop!" She turned around and said "Papa, I have the dough but am wondering what to buy!" Mahesh remarked "What to buy or what not to buy?" Shagun had a childish grin on her face and said "You know I am from the fashion world and have become selective now. Money is not the issue!"

Priti, on the hand, had by now disappeared and was busy looking up some clothes for Kiran. Mahesh had to make some effort to look for her. He was finally successful and told her "Priti, why don't you also look up something for Shagun?" In response she was quizzical and said "Its been years since I looked up something for Shagun! Why are you asking this?" Mahesh gave a bewildered look and said "She appears to be disinterested for a change! I feel that she is perhaps hesitating to take money from me, unlike before!" Priti joined Shagun and recommended some dresses to her.

In response, she was surprised to hear her saying "Mom I already have lots like them. I do not want to duplicate and waste money unnecessarily." Mom was aghast! This is the same Shagun who never used to bother about similarity in dresses as long as she liked them. Finally, she bought a few dresses and the family proceeded to see different locations and sightseeing spots in Phuket.

They stopped for a bite in between and finally went back to the hotel. While relaxing in the room Priti mentioned "The atmosphere is so peaceful unlike earlier when Shagun used to be upset with us on some count or the other. Remember our trip to Goa and what all happened there!" Mahesh remarked "Shagun is upto something as her behaviour is in sharp contrast to earlier times. Maybe, she has liked a boy and is waiting for the right time to tell us and is trying hard to create a congenial atmosphere within the family lest we may end up arguing with her especially after her recent breakup in her first friendship."

Priti was in denial and said "I am her mother and if that had been the case I would figured it out. It is something else and sooner or later we would have to talk to her about it. I am quite positive about this!" Mahesh was impressed and said that he was pleasantly surprised about her clarity of mind. In the late evening they went out for dinner and had typical Thai food. Priti told Shagun to decide on the order.

Shagun was all smiles and said "Okay, I will decide but I need your inputs on the selection of the dishes." Her mother understood and suggested a few dishes. She asked papa if he was interested in a drink. Papa promptly replied in the affirmative. While Mahesh had a couple of whiskies, the ladies had a glass of red wine each. By the time, the family members were through with their drinks, they were a wee bit tipsy and were feeling lightheaded.

Mahesh remarked "Shagun, you have become a sweet and obedient daughter, making me proud of you. I wish all these years which have passed by had been the way it is now. Life would have been more enjoyable!" Shagun replied "I was testing your parental patience! Having done so, I felt that it was now time that you see my better side. So now I will be at your beck and call!"

Priti was by now laughing and said "Great! We have something in common! You know, we were doing the same as parents. However, there is a difference here! We were and are and will always be there for you!" Shagun smiled and said "Mom and dad, I will over the years be at par with your expectations in every possible way" the parents could not help feeling a trifle emotional and Mahesh said "I had a satisfying family meal after a long time! All thanks to Shagun to have made it possible." They finally went back to their resort to have a good night's sleep. Kiran, too, was all pepped up seeing the mood of the family.

The next day they left for Bangkok to spend three days there as well. Their hotel was located in the heart of a market area making the place very lively. The first day was spent in sightseeing and witnessing some spectacular stage shows. They dined in an area by the name of china town where one gets the unique privilege of sitting on the streetside and having a meal. It was a satisfying day and the family thoroughly enjoyed themselves.

The next day started with a massage in one of the parlours close to the hotel, with all of them feeling relaxed and rejuvenated. Bangkok was particularly known for a couple of malls specifically for shopping of all kinds. They went there but much to the surprise and astonishment of both Mahesh and Priti, Shagun was highly selective of her garments, despite Priti asking her if she needed any money. Shagun did not take any nor did she splurge on the garments on display there.

The food in all the joints was exceedingly tasty and to the liking of the family. The weather was warm and hence the need for airconditioning was there all the time. In between, in the afternoon, on one of the three days Shagun took Kiran in the market adjacent to the hotel and bought her a few purses, handkerchief sets, two things which she is particularly fond of. She got her hand and face lotion each and by the time they came back to the hotel, Kiran was delirious with joy.

Such was the level of excitement, that Kiran decided to wake up her parents in the adjacent room just to show to them what her sister had got for her. Seeing the happy faces of her family Shagun was thrilled too as her newly adopted strategy of self improvement through introspection was doing wonders and making her happy perpetually.

That evening, while having tea in their room Priti mentioned to Mahesh "Don't you think that we ought to talk to Shagun and quiz her on her hidden agenda, though in a positive way. I am not strategising but you will agree that there is a sea-change in her, in such a short span of time. It is too good to accept that all of a sudden the texture of our relationships had changed so quickly and comprehensively." Mahesh pondered and replied pensively "I agree. Something has definitely happened to have impacted her, to such an extent! She is talking sense all the time! She is trying to make us happy all the time. Lets nicely engage her in a conversation and find out the reality."

The children were in the next room and Priti promptly called them on the intercom and asked them to come over to their room. The children were now in their room and Priti did not waste any further time and straightaway came to the point.

She asked Shagun "It is now time that you tell us the reason behind this radical change in your mannerisms, behaviour, infact the look on your face which too has become pleasant unlike the disgruntled look we were used to over the last several years." Mahesh was keenly observing his elder daughter for any clues but there were none, barring the sweet and attractive look on her face, making her a completely different person from ever before.

Kiran at this crucial juncture chipped in "Sis, do not hide! Tell them the truth." Hearing this, Shagun smiled and looked affectionately at her parents. She replied "I am copying you, you both have been trying to be very nice and sweet to me. I am doing the same! Reciprocating niceness with sweetness!" The parents did not understand! They decided to probe further, and asked "Look you are being vague! Surely, you have been in touch with somebody who has advised you to do so and you are, perhaps, acting on his/her advice!"

Shagun was amused and was having fun at the nature of the communication. She said "You are right, mom and dad! I had a hearty chat with one of my close friends who told me. Let me now not beat around the bush! It is all about "self change through introspection and inner realisation" I am convinced about its practical relevance and resulting benefits."

The parents were thrilled and a wave of uncanny happiness filled their minds and hearts. So, they realised that Shagun was on the same path. Truly amazing! Priti finally spoke "You know, we have been applying this process in our daily lives and have experienced the associated benefits in terms of happiness and how to handle our day to day problems and confront and successfully overcome them." Shagun then narrated how she had started applying this thought process on a daily basis and felt good in doing so.

Mahesh mentioned "The same process can be followed in negative and adverse circumstances also. I have tried to do so and you feel more confident and also get appreciation as a bonus." Priti remarked "It attracts people to you as they start seeing the difference in you." The parents got up and gave her a hug! Kiran was clapping and was understandably happy at this sight of a reunion of sorts between her sister and her parents.

The family was now scheduled to visit Pattaya, a famous tourist destination in Thailand which was about 2hrs away from Bangkok. The place was buzzing with activity, with visitors from all parts of the world. The well known walking street in Pattaya alongside a beautiful beach overlooking the sea was a treat to watch! The beachside was lined with numerous multi-cuisine restaurants and eating joints.

The family enjoyed their last two days in Pattaya to the hilt with their newly acquired bonding which was missing over the years. The parents and Shagun had resolved that they would try their level best to strengthen this bond which now existed amongst them and make up for Kiran's lost childhood and set an example for others to sort out their lives, for the better. They went back to their home thoroughly satisfied with the outcome of the vacation.

Mahesh and Shagun got into their routines while Priti got busy with her routine with Kiran already showing signs of substantial improvement in terms of her wellbeing, despite her disabilities, merely because of the change in the environment in the house, with a sense of peace and equanimity. The parents were now looking forward to a suitable match for Shagun and had left the decision making to her. A unique level of understanding was developing between the parents and the children, a chord of understanding which was solidifying day by day.

The readers may note the sequence of events in the family's life, right from the beginning, with recaps in between. The process of self change is possible only through a deep introspection and acceptance of the responsibility for one's own circumstances and a dedicated effort to improve one's own life through self improvement thereby making the external environment conducive as well.